Style 101

WHAT EVERY STYLISH
WOMAN SHOULD KNOW

fashion 👜 beauty 💄 home 🪑 entertaining 🍸

IN STYLE

Managing Editor Charla Lawhon
Executive Editors
Martha McCully, Leonora Wiener
Assistant Managing Editor Patrick Moffitt
Deputy Editors
Alison Gwinn, Donna Bulseco
Editorial Operations Director Lavinel Savu
Fashion Directors
Hal Rubenstein, Cynthia Weber Cleary
Beauty Director Amy Synnott-D'Annibale
Senior Beauty Editor Jennifer Tung
Beauty Editor Ning Chao
Creative Director John Korpics
Photography Director Alix B. Campbell

Publisher Lynette Harrison Brubaker
General Manager Maria Tucci Beckett

Editor, *Style 101* Alison Gwinn
Editorial Assistant Rebecca Grice
Imaging Manager Steve Cadicamo
Imaging Specialist Rey Delgado
Production Associate Bijal Saraiya

TIME INC. HOME ENTERTAINMENT

Publisher
Richard Fraiman
General Manager
Steven Sandonato
Executive Director, Marketing Services
Carol Pittard
Director, Retail & Special Sales
Tom Mifsud
Director, New Product Development
Peter Harper
Assistant Director, Brand Marketing
Laura Adam
Assistant General Counsel
Dasha Smith Dwin
Book Production Manager
Suzanne Janso
Marketing Manager
Victoria Alfonso
Prepress Manager
Anne-Michelle Gallero

MELCHER MEDIA

This book was produced by
Melcher Media, Inc.
124 West 13th St.
New York, NY 10011
www.melcher.com

Publisher Charles Melcher
Associate Publisher Bonnie Eldon
Editor in Chief Duncan Bock

Senior Editor/Project Manager
Lia Ronnen
Assistant Editor Lauren Nathan
Design Studiousher.com
Art Director Naomi Usher
Production Director Kurt Andrews
Cover Art/Icons Bee: Larkworthy.com
Copy Editor Heidi Ernst

PUBLISHED BY IN STYLE BOOKS

Photography © 2007
photographers listed on final pages
© 2007 Time Inc. Home Entertainment
1271 Avenue of the Americas
New York, NY 10020

ISBN 13: 978-1-933821-88-7
ISBN 10: 1-933821-88-4
Library of Congress Control
Number: 2007904276

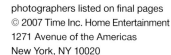

Style101

WHAT EVERY STYLISH
WOMAN SHOULD KNOW

from the editors of *In Style*

edited by alison gwinn

written by kathleen fifield

designed by studio usher

PRODUCED BY  **MELCHER MEDIA** **FOR** InStyle Books **AND** Time Inc. HOME ENTERTAINMENT

contents

how to: home

how to: entertaining

credits/acknowledgments

how to: **use this book**

blue = home / green = entertaining / **purple = fashion** / orange = beauty

USE IT WHEN PANIC SETS IN. Don't know what to wear to that black-tie-optional wedding in Houston? Or which hostess gift says, Thanks for inviting me to your sumptuous new country house and sorry I ruined your espresso machine? Or how to stock a bar for last-minute cocktails for 50? Relax. Take a deep breath, pour yourself some water, and down a couple of our reassuringly simple capsule-size chapters. Drawn from the best of *In Style* magazine, we offer how-tos on everything from your wardrobe to your decor, in an order as random as what life throws at you.

USE IT WHEN INSPIRATION FAILS. There are times when a day of shopping with a friend is the perfect diversion. And there are times when the artificial light of the mall seems to cast a pall over everything and you find yourself muttering: *Um, what am I looking for again? And how much should I spend on it? And will it make my arms look fat?* We've been there. So we tried to make our odes to shopping (and primping, and getting in shape, and reorganizing the closet) as encouraging as ... well, if not sunshine through the clouds, then unexpected weight loss or a perfect, glowing complexion before a big night out.

USE IT WHEN YOU MISS THAT CLASS. No, not the one called "Cross-Cultural Ironies in 1920s Fashion" or "Bankruptcy Through Beauty Products." The one where they just tell you in simple terms how to find flattering jeans, blow out your hair, apply concealer or shape your brows. With our easy step-by-step guides to getting gorgeous, you'll be able to perfect your technique in no time — with little or no fuss.

USE IT WHEN YOU NEED A SHOT IN THE ARM. Life can be hard. Which means things like entertaining your friends or buying a sofa should be fun. So open up this book to any page and inside you'll find smart advice and useful suggestions that will make your life a little easier — and a lot more stylish.

how to: **find an ideal lipstick**

THE NEWS IN HUES Lipstick, like clothing, has become seasonless; matching your own coloring is the goal now. Roughly, cooler tones (those on the bluer end of the spectrum) work better for fairer skin, and warmer tones (those closer to red and orange) work best for darker skin. Say you're trying to choose a shade of pink: A warm pink is peachy; a cool pink is more mauve. Or try a shade that pros say looks beautiful on nearly everyone: a sheer berry, a subtle pink, or a light brown or nude spiked with gold, bronze or red.

PERFECT TIMING Choose your color for different times of day. From 9 to 5, warm and creamy shades (more pink, less red) will look best, especially under harsh office lights. Evening light is more forgiving, so smooth on the sheer fuchsia (for fair skin) or brick red (for olive).

MATTE OR SHEER? The formula—gloss, stain, sheer or matte—matters too. Generally, the wetter the texture, the less long-wearing but more goof-proof. We all know how easy it is to spread on some gloss and go—and how quickly it disappears from our lips. A drier stain grips and holds, so you have to be exacting about applying it within the lines. Something in the middle is best for day: A sheer lipstick is more permanent than gloss but easier to apply than a matte or stain. Save the heavy gloss, and the shimmery stuff, for night.

MIX MASTER A final pointer: Combining one part lipstick, one part gloss to create a custom color is an inexpensive way to broaden your lip wardrobe. Brighten a brown stick with a dab of pink gloss, or lighten a dark shade with clear gloss.

 DID YOU KNOW? The average woman consumes 6 lbs. of lipstick in a lifetime.

how to: **shop smart**

1   **KNOW WHAT YOU NEED** Always have a list. It can be in your head or on paper, but the point is to zero in on what you need so you're not overwhelmed at the mall.

2   **BE SURE ABOUT IT** Ask yourself, "Do I love it? Does it look great on me? Will I wear it?" And don't buy it unless the answer is an emphatic yes.

3   **DRESS FOR ACTION** Wear clothes that are easy to get into and out of and shoes that slip on. And you'll be happier if you put on a little makeup.

4   **BUY CLASSICS** Don't feel guilty about spending more for classic pieces such as wool trousers, pumps or a leather handbag. Spend less on trendier items.

5   **AMORTIZE THE COSTS** Is the $1,000 coat way too much or within reason? Calculate the cost per wear and factor in how many seasons you might wear it.

6 **AVOID THE CROWDS** If you can sacrifice a weekday morning for shopping (before the lunch rush), you'll be rewarded with emptier stores and less harried salespeople.

7 **MIX AND MATCH** Style today is often more about mixing and matching than outfits. Try buying pieces that work together to solve the "What do I wear this with?" question.

8 **KNOW YOURSELF** Be honest about what styles flatter your body type best and are appropriate for your age. And always shop for the size you are now.

9 **FEEL CHIPPER** Don't shop when you're really hungry or really tired—or when you have only two hours to find something to wear to a party.

10 **GO WITH NEUTRALS** When buying inexpensive items, stick with neutral colors since cheap fabrics look that way in bright shades.

how to: **arrange flowers**

ROUND VASE

This is perfect for roses, which look best in a container that mirrors their shape and that is opaque. Cut fresh roses at a sharp angle and place them briefly in hot water, then put them in a vase filled with water at room temperature. Round vases also work well for carnations, anemones or ranunculus.

BUD VASE

Poppies are lightweight and have artfully curved stems; a dainty bud vase will hold the blossom upright and let it do its thing. For an easy centerpiece, group together three bud vases of varying shapes. Freesia, sweet peas and gerbera daisies are also attractive in bud vases.

JULEP CUP

A delicate flower such as a grape hyacinth matches this petite container. The straight sides of the cup provide a sturdy anchor for spindly stems. Other options are lilies of the valley, snowdrops and sweet peas. Most cut flowers should be one and a half to two times the height of the vase.

BOWL

Float one peony in a low, wide bowl in a bathroom or on a bedside table. The lush bloom against the spare backdrop has a modern and serene appeal. A drop of bleach helps keep the water clean, but you should still change it daily. Camellias and gardenias are also appropriate in this container.

CYLINDER

For long, flowering branches, such as quince, you need something tall. The narrow shape also helps anchor the stems. Cut into the bottom ends of branches with clippers to help them take in water more easily. Other suitable branches for cylinders are cherry, apple, lilac and forsythia.

URN

Dense flowers with large blossoms and long, supple stems, such as tulips, complement the urn's heavier shape beautifully. And the flexible stems let flowers stretch along the lip of an urn like outspread arms. Hyacinth and viburnum are also great options for these vintage vessels.

how to: create a smoky eye

HIGHLIGHT

Prep with a foundation over the entire lid. Then, using a soft eye-shadow brush, apply a shimmery shadow in a neutral shade, such as bronze, to the entire lid. Layer on a medium-tone shadow (gray is the classic choice) from your lash line to the crease.

LINE

Using a small, firm brush (and light, feathery strokes), trace around eyes with a dark matte shadow and blend it into the existing medium tone on your lid. If a smoky gray is too dark, try a deep green for brown eyes, or brown or taupe for blue eyes. For extra oomph use a black eye pencil on top and bottom lash lines, and blend, blend, blend.

LIGHTEN

For a finishing touch try lightening up a little: A pale, shimmery shadow on the inner corners of your eyes will make them look open and awake. Take a small brush and highlight a V-shaped section on the inner corners and blend. If necessary touch up with foundation. Add two coats of mascara.

how to: **walk in high heels**

1   **PUT HEAD UP, SHOULDERS BACK** Heels tend to pitch your weight forward, so straightening up—and tightening your core—will offset some of the pressure on your feet.

2   **TAKE BABY STEPS** Striding in a normal heel-to-toe motion can snap a stiletto. When you're elevated take short steps, going down evenly on the ball of the foot and heel.

3   **SPREAD 'EM** As your weight shifts fully onto a foot, splay your toes in the shoe slightly; this will help to distribute the weight onto the ball of the foot.

4   **GET HIPPY** When you're feeling off-balance, you tend to stiffen up. For an easier momentum swing your hips in small, sideways, figure-eight motions.

5   **SHOP SMARTER** When scouting for your next set of heels, know that the farther forward the arch, the less you will teeter-totter.

how to: **set up a basic bar**

CHECKLIST FOR A BASIC BAR FOR 50

alcohol
- ☐ rum, one quart
- ☐ vodka, two quarts
- ☐ whiskey, one quart
- ☐ tequila, one quart
- ☐ gin, one quart
- ☐ dry vermouth, one bottle

juices, one quart each
- ☐ orange
- ☐ cranberry

sodas, six liters each
- ☐ cola
- ☐ ginger ale
- ☐ club soda

other mixers
- ☐ tonic water, six liters
- ☐ seltzer, six liters
- ☐ Rose's lime juice, one bottle
- ☐ Tabasco sauce, one bottle

wine, ten bottles each
- ☐ red
- ☐ white

ice
- ☐ ten 5 lb. bags

garnishes
- ☐ ten lemons
- ☐ ten limes
- ☐ ten oranges
- ☐ green olives, one jar

equipment
- ☐ bar spoon
- ☐ bar towels
- ☐ bottle opener
- ☐ bowls and glasses to hold garnishes
- ☐ cocktail napkins
- ☐ cocktail or Boston shaker
- ☐ corkscrew
- ☐ cutting board
- ☐ ice bucket
- ☐ ice-filled coolers for wine and beer
- ☐ ice tongs or scoop
- ☐ mixing glasses
- ☐ paring knife
- ☐ straws
- ☐ trash container
- ☐ tub or tray to hold used glassware
- ☐ tub to hold extra ice

how to: **find jeans that fit**

DENIM It's not all about stretch. The tight weave of premium denim goes far to prevent that annoying second-day sag, which can cause your jeans to seem a size larger overnight.

WAISTBAND A wider waistband can flatter a slightly fuller tummy. With others, watch that you don't have a sausage effect around a tight waist.

RISE Otherwise known as crotch length. Superlow styles may wax and wane. Aim for a style that's solidly below your belly button.

SLOPE The relationship between the front rise and the back rise is an important part of fit. The right one can give you a flattering low look in front and thong coverage in back.

HEM A slight flare is easiest for most body types; it will balance out wider hips.

WASH The process of washing—and bleaching, grinding and sanding—denim is always evolving. Avoid details in places where you don't want attention, and skip pairs with too many obvious fireworks.

POCKETS Their size and placement can make all the difference in the rear view: If they're small and far apart, for instance, your caboose might look wider.

YOKE It's that V-shaped double seam below the waistband and above pockets. Pairs that downplay or eliminate it can flatter larger or saggier derrières.

SIDE POCKETS Make sure there's no unflattering, hip-widening gap here.

LENGTH Leave 'em longer to elongate the legs or if you'll be wearing heels regularly with this pair. Cuffs work with cropped jeans.

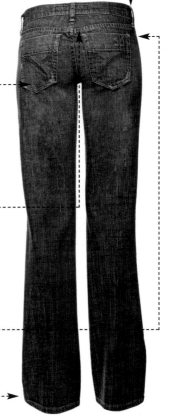

quick: tip

GET SMOOTH AND SHINY HAIR For deep hydration, look for a conditioner with a high level of acetyl alcohol—an ultrarich fatty acid that helps retain moisture. For a salon-worthy treatment at home, comb moisturizer through damp hair, blast sections of your hair with a blow-dryer for several seconds, and rinse. To tame flyaways and frizz: Spray the palms of your hands with hairspray, then run them over your hair.

how to: **battle a breakout**

bummer: **flaking blemish**

Resist the urge to remove skin as it flakes. Instead, rub a bit of creamy cleanser onto the pimple in a circular motion. Dab on a 1 percent hydro-cortisone cream to further calm skin, then apply a creamy concealer and powder to set the coverage.

bummer: **pimple forming**

When you feel that unwanted pressure under the skin, wrap an ice cube in a paper towel and apply to the affected area for 20 minutes. Repeat two to three times during the day. Essential oils such as tea-tree oil, which are absorbed into the skin, can also be soothing.

bummer: **cold sores on your lip**

The herpes simplex virus causes them, but sun and stress are the pri-mary triggers of outbreaks. If you can't stay out of the sun, slather lips (in-cluding the outer corners) with a physical sunblock that has zinc oxide.

bummer: **a zit before a big event**

Visiting a dermatologist for a cortisone injection can make an unwanted lump vanish in about a day. Or apply a hot compress to help it dissipate more quickly. Dabbing on a topical hydrocortisone cream like Cortaid can also help, as can ingredients like sulfur and calamine. During the day camouflage with a concealer that contains pore-cleansing salicylic acid.

bummer: **woke up with one**

The immediate fix is to use a drop of tea-tree oil, then apply ice wrapped in a washcloth followed by a topical hydrocortisone cream. A bigger fix: Switch to a night cream that's not as heavy, and avoid greasy hair prod-ucts. Sleep on your back; lying on your face can cause flare-ups.

how to: **buy gold**

BY THE NUMBERS Karats (as opposed to carats, which measure a gem's weight) measure the gold content of a piece. In general, the higher the karat, the higher the price. On fine jewelry a stamp reading "14kt" (58.3 percent gold) or "18kt" (75 percent gold), for instance, should appear on the back of a piece. (Europe uses only 18kt, and the stamp reads ".750.") If a piece is too small for a stamp, have the store guarantee karat weight and note it on the receipt.

THE CLASSIC PICK Yellow is the natural color of gold—and the most popular. The metal is also incredibly malleable, which means it can be woven or finished in a delicate filigree. Different karat weights of yellow gold have slightly different appearances: 14kt gold is bright and sunny; 18kt has a soft, warm tone and is the most commonly used color today. The rarely used 22kt is deep and rich, with an almost antique appearance. And 24kt gold is almost 100 percent pure; it has a rich orange glow. But beware: Since there is only a trace of alloy to strengthen it, it is quite soft and scratches easily.

GETTING COOLER/WARMER If you look better in cool tones, the icy cast of white gold will be the most flattering metal for you. In comparison to other white metals, white gold has a richer look than silver and costs up to 30 percent less than platinum. A combination of yellow gold and white metals, it's primarily made in 14kt or 18kt. Many white-gold pieces are plated with rhodium (a shiny white metal) to add brilliance and prevent the metal from darkening. If warmer tones make your skin and eyes perk up, stick with yellow gold or try pink gold, which is a mixture of yellow gold and copper. This color was popular in the Victorian era and again in the U.S. during the 1940s; there was a shortage of platinum during the war, so gold jewelry in general was particularly in vogue.

how to: **buy silver**

1 **GO OUNCE FOR OUNCE** Compared with gold, silver is affordable—50 times as affordable. You can expect to pay around $13.50 an ounce for silver, which is about four times what it cost five years ago.

2 **CONSIDER CRAFTSMANSHIP** The cost of sterling-silver jewelry is determined by how much labor it requires. The price increases if both machine and handwork is done and is even higher if the piece is entirely handmade.

3 **FIND THE STAMP** Sterling silver is an alloy of 92.5 percent silver and 7.5 percent copper. When shopping for jewelry, look for a stamp that says "sterling" or ".925." A designer's stamp may appear as well.

4 **CHECK THE FINISH** Whatever its quality, silver will inevitably tarnish. But some designers deliberately tarnish pieces in the manufacturing process, often to highlight details.

how to: **make over your desk**

1   **DRESS UP THE DESKTOP** Must-have accessories? A flexible lamp, clock, framed personal photo and vase of flowers. Mix textures and colors to add visual interest.

2   **STOCK THE DRAWERS** Outfit them with trays and fill with paper clips, scissors, rubber bands and stationery. Stash lesser-used items in a nearby closet.

3   **PERSONALIZE** Make your workspace an extension of your home. Choose a desk that feels like furniture but has ample room to work and deep drawers.

4   **FILE IT AWAY** To keep the desktop clean, you have to be disciplined with your filing cabinet. Shred outdated info, file what's necessary, and purge at least once a year.

5   **CONTROL KEEPSAKES** Look at personal photos with a trashcan nearby and toss unwanted shots immediately. If you can't place them in albums, put them in photo boxes.

how to: **pick a makeup brush**

1 POWDER Large with soft, natural bristles. Dip into loose or pressed powder, shake off excess, and dust over skin to set foundation.

2 FOUNDATION Use this flat, firm brush with (preferably) synthetic bristles to apply foundation, using short downward strokes from forehead to chin.

3 CONCEALER To deposit cover-up just where you want it, use a small, flat, blunt-edge version with synthetic bristles.

4 EYE SHADOW Sweep shadow on lids and highlighter on brow bones with brush's flat sides; use the tip to define creases.

5 HIGHLIGHTER The fine, feather-light design works to dust subtle, glittery highlights on cheekbones for evenings out.

6 LIQUID EYELINER Better than other applicators for applying fast-setting liquid or cream liners along the lash line.

7 LIP You want it firm but flexible to place color precisely. Choose a rounded or flat-tip version—your choice.

8 SHADOW EYELINER This is small and firm, with bristles and a slightly rounded tip for smudging the line once you draw it.

9 BLUSH Look for a size as big as the apple of your cheek. The rounded shape and fluffy bristles make for easy blending (read: no clown face).

10 BROW You want a stiff, angled version to fill in sparse brows with dots of eye shadow.

POWDER

paula dorf

MADE IN JAPAN

Trish McEvoy · BEA

NARS

① ② ③ ④ ⑤ ⑥ ⑦ ⑧ ⑨ ⑩

how to: **create perfect lips**

LINE

Choose a liner that's close to your own lip color, not the shade of your lipstick. Outline edges while holding the pencil at an angle, and line from the outer corners toward the center. Then use soft, featherlike strokes to fill in the entire lip. Finally, dab with a sponge before applying lipstick.

FILL

Dark and matte colors in particular should be precisely applied. Start at the center of your mouth and blend outward with a lip brush. Blot lips with a tissue, dust with translucent powder, then apply a second coat. Or for a casual look with just a hint of color, lightly dab lipstick on with your finger.

FINISH

Paint around the perimeter of your lip line with a bit of concealer to prevent color from bleeding. To thin out the color, blend a waxy balm on top of lipstick. A transparent gloss on top will create a brighter shine. To make lips look fuller, apply a dab of shimmery gloss to the center of your bottom lip.

how to: **make your shoes last**

LEATHER Softer leather requires a cream polish; heavier leathers can take a wax polish, which serves the same water-repelling function that a silicone spray does for suede and cloth.

LINING If the lining of a shoe comes out, you can glue it down with rubber cement.

HEEL Replace heel tips as necessary. Subbing in rubber tips for plastic ones can make for a softer walk. If you've worn through the tip into the heel itself, you can also have that replaced.

SOLE If it's hard and slick, have a shoe repairer add a thin rubber sole (or half sole, for pumps) for comfort, traction and longevity.

TOE BOX If you've worn the shoe and it still feels tight, have it stretched by a shoe repairer (who can also stretch or shorten straps).

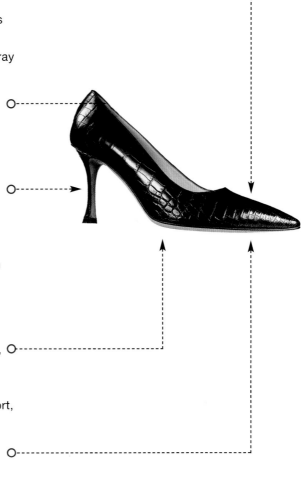

how to: **buy cashmere**

1 **KNOW YOUR FIBERS** The best fibers—the finest hairs hand-harvested from the bellies and chins of high-altitude goats (they're called kashmiri) only once a year—are spun into the best yarn and sweaters. You know 'em when you feel them. And while these shorter, finer hairs up the price significantly, they're less likely to pill than coarser hairs.

2 **IS THERE OOMPH?** A great cashmere sweater should have a slight spring, what those in the biz call loft. To test the strength of the weave, pull the sides of the sweater apart and let them go. Does it spring back into shape?

3 **LOOK FOR BRIGHT COLORS** If you're eyeing a navy or black piece, check that it's as soft as the baby pinks on the shelf. Sometimes a lower grade of cashmere is used in sweaters that are dyed darker. But it's hard to get lower grades of goat hair to dye well, so a bright, consistent color (especially in pastel sweaters) costs more to produce and is a sign of quality.

4 **IS IT HANDKNITTED?** A $500 sweater will be knit entirely by hand (you'll notice cuffs are identical inside and out). Cheaper versions are lockstitched; that is, panels are sewn together by machine.

5 **WHAT ABOUT BLENDS?** Read the label; the most expensive options should be 100 percent cashmere. A cheaper blend should have at least 10 percent cashmere. Also note how well the label is sewn on; sometimes that reflects the care taken with the garment overall. Another good sign? If it's knit in Scotland or Italy.

6 **CHECK PLY AND GAUGE** Ply is the number of strands twisted together to achieve thickness. The higher the ply, the more substantial the feel. Gauge is how tightly those strands are twisted. Cashmere can work for all seasons, depending on ply and gauge.

7 **THE ONE FOR YOU** When buying an investment sweater, make sure to keep figure issues in mind. V-necks and crewnecks are universally flattering. Turtlenecks can elongate the torso for short waists. Boatnecks help balance larger hips. Neutrals like gray or tan have the longest style longevity.

how to: **eat right for your skin**

PROBLEM	WHAT TO EAT	WHAT TO AVOID
ACNE-PRONE >>>		
	Bright red and orange fruits and vegetables are rich in beta-carotene, which the body converts to oil-reducing vitamin A.	Iodine-rich salt, shrimp and sea-weed stimulate oil glands, causing irritation of pores. Pure chocolate is safe, but sugary desserts are not.
WRINKLES >>>		
	Fruits rich in color (such as berries) have vitamin C, which promotes anti-aging, skin-firming collagen and antioxidants.	Watch your sugar intake (it can lead to sagging) and avoid taking too much iron (high doses may contribute to wrinkles).
DRY SKIN >>>		
	Drink lots of water and eat foods with good fats (which help keep cell walls strong and prevent water loss), like avocado and olive oil.	Coffee and black tea dehydrate your internal tissues and skin. Margarine and most fried foods can deplete levels of good fats and cause dry skin.

PROBLEM	WHAT TO EAT	WHAT TO AVOID

ROSACEA/REDNESS >>>>>>>>>>>>>>>>>>>>>>>>>>>>>>>>>>>>>>>

Eat calming foods such as fish, cucumbers and licorice. Also, turmeric seasoning is high in curcumin, an antioxidant and anti-inflammatory.

Hot foods (in temperature or spiciness), alcohol and caffeine make blood vessels swell, so skin looks redder, according to dermatologists.

BROWN SPOTS >>

Powerful antioxidants (found in dark chocolate, pomegranates and broccoli) that fight sun damage are your best beauty bets.

Alcohol, especially beer, as well as processed foods, weaken the immune system, making skin more sensitive to sunlight.

DULL SKIN >>

Green and orange veggies increase vitamin A levels, making skin cells shed faster for a radiant complexion. Eating yams can add luster to your skin.

Spices, garlic and onions increase circulation and impart a healthy glow, but don't overdose on them or you'll end up red in the face.

quick: tip

KEEP WRINKLES AT BAY To get more bang for your beauty buck, look for antiaging products in serum form. These lightweight liquids tend to pack more potent levels of antioxidants, firming agents and skin brighteners than rich lotions do. They're also more easily absorbed, which increases their effectiveness.

how to: **find a bra that fits**

problem: **fuzzy numbers**

If you can't get a grip on whether you're a 36B or 34C, ask for a professional fitting at the store. A good salesperson might also be able to steer you toward the best brand for you, since sizing varies by manufacturer.

problem: **in-between band sizes**

Ideally, a bra should initially feel right on the loosest size setting, since bras can stretch up to two inches in the back with wear and washing. Also know that as you go up in band size, the cup size gets slightly larger too, which means you may need to try a smaller cup if your band size grows.

problem: **falling-down straps**

First off, you should adjust them every time you wear the bra, since straps start to loosen over time. They're at the correct length if your bra is level across your back and not too tight when using the middle hooks. If straps keep falling down at this length, the culprit might be a too-big band.

problem: **crinkly cups**

If you're having this issue with a new bra, try getting into it this way: Lean over, jiggle a bit, and let your breasts "fall" into the cups. If that doesn't fix the wrinkling, you may need to go down one band size. In general breasts should fill up both the top and bottom portion of the cup.

problem: **spillage**

Busting out over the sides or tops of cups is a classic indication you need to go up a cup size. Another clue? An underwire that doesn't lie flat or that pokes into the breast tissue; it should fit comfortably around the breasts and not lie on top of them at all. In fact, in the right bra for you, you should hardly be aware of the underwire at all.

how to: **set up a buffet**

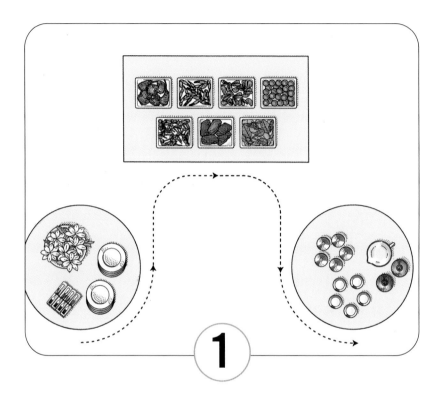

Big buffets will flow more smoothly if they're organized on multiple tables, with enough space among them to avoid crowding. Set up cutlery, food and drinks so that guests can proceed in an orderly way and not have to back-track: Plates at the beginning, glasses at the end alongside drinks. To make it easier for guests to carry utensils, try rolling them inside napkins rather than setting them out individually. If possible, serve food that doesn't require cut-ting so you can eliminate the need for knives and dining tabletops.

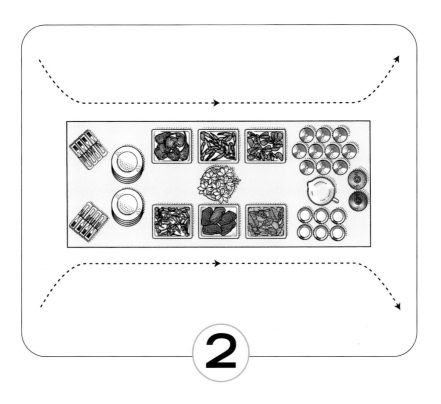

FOR SMALL PARTIES

If your buffet is relatively small and casual, you can set up everything on a single table—though it's best if guests can approach it from either side. The flow is the same as with larger groups: utensils, food, glassware. To add some visual interest, set the food at varying heights and include an accent like a pretty candelabra or flowers. Unlike table flowers, which need to be low enough to encourage conversation, buffet-table centerpieces can be tall and dramatic.

how to: **undo a beauty mishap**

mishap: **too much blush**

Sprinkle translucent powder on a makeup sponge and blend over the too-bright color. The trick is to blend the color in toward the apple of the cheeks instead of out toward your ears. If cheeks still look too intense, go over them again with two drops of foundation on a makeup wedge.

mishap: **eyebrow gap**

To fill an undesired void, brush brow hairs in the opposite direction of growth so the bare area becomes more visible, then use an ultrafine brow pencil to cover it with light, hair-length strokes. Finally, brush the brow back into place.

mishap: **streaky self-tanner**

To soften too much color in one spot, stroke the area with a lemon wedge (citric acid is a natural exfoliant) or a cotton ball soaked in hydrogen per-oxide. To fill in light streaks, even out color by applying tinted self-tanner with the edge of a makeup wedge, or brush on matte bronzer with a small blush brush.

mishap: **perfume overdose**

To remove a fragrance's concentrated oil base, rub skin with an un-scented baby wipe or a cotton ball soaked in rubbing alcohol. To vaporize a scent that you've oversprayed on clothing, blast fabric with a hair dryer for 30 seconds.

mishap: **too-light highlights**

It's best to have your colorist correct truly bungled highlights, but while you wait for an appointment, wash your hair twice with a caramel-hued color-depositing shampoo to deepen highlights and add a rich color.

mishap: **too-short bangs**

Weigh the hair down by dampening it and adding gel, then comb to one side and secure with a bobby pin (or two; you want the bangs to recede into your hairline, not to fall straight from the pin). If some of the skimpy fringe won't reach to the side, try adjusting your part slightly toward the center and combing the rest of the bangs to the opposite side.

mishap: **stiff hairspray**

Use a wide-tooth comb on small sections of hair, starting at the ends and working up to the roots. Rub a dime-size dollop of hand cream between your hands and run your fingers through the over-sprayed spot to take away the crackle and add moisture. Shake your head upside down afterward, since some cheaper sprays flake once the formula is broken up.

mishap: **product overload**

Went a little heavy with the styling serum? Dust your hands with baby powder, rub them together well, and scrunch the greasy section. The same process also works with a dry shampoo.

mishap: **smudged polish**

Dip the pad of a finger from the opposite hand into nail polish remover and gently blend away the smear with your finger. Add a coat of clear polish instead of more color (which would make that nail darker than the others).

mishap: **clumpy mascara**

Act immediately, since mascara is formulated to dry in seconds. Wipe all the formula off your mascara wand with a piece of paper napkin or paper towel (not a tissue, which may shed) and wiggle the wand gently from side to side, from the roots to the tips of lashes.

how to: **control clutter**

1 VISUALIZE Imagine your house filled with things you love to look
at (and not mounds of clutter). Imagine knowing instantly where
something is located when you need it (without rooting through
the junk drawer). Feeling motivated?

2 THROW STUFF OUT The next step to making the harmony happen is being ruthless about pitching things you're not using and don't love. Make up rules if you have to: Throw out magazines you haven't read in a month or clothes you haven't worn in a year.

3 MOVE THINGS AROUND Go about your routine for a week and notice if the things you use every day are easily accessible. Why are you stashing your hair dryer on the lowest shelf of your linen closet when it's a pain to reach down to retrieve it every morning? Jot down what needs to be moved and take a Saturday to do it.

4 KNOW YOUR WEAKNESSES Understand your own biggest bugaboo and find an easy, fail-safe and visually pleasing solution. If you can never find your keys when you need them, install a sleek shelf by your door. Place a beautiful bowl atop it. Drop in keys.

5 ADD STORAGE The three rules to getting organized: containers, containers, containers. Whether woven baskets, canvas boxes or clear tubs, buy extras of them and use to hold like with like.

6 LIGHTEN UP Consider lighting some cupboards. You can buy inexpensive battery-operated fixtures at a hardware store and attach them to a cabinet door or wall.

7 GET MAIL UNDER CONTROL Battling clutter daily means dealing with the incoming mail every day. Open it with a wastebasket and shredder nearby so you can complete the task in one sitting.

8 RELAX! Finally, give yourself a break once in a while. If you honestly can't decide whether to keep some could-be clutter, box it up and set it aside, but flag it with a date. If you haven't come back to it within the year, chances are it should go to Goodwill.

how to: **find perfect pants**

(1)

CLASSIC

With their flat front, slightly flared legs and overall streamlined silhouette, classic pants are unshakably chic. Play up their masculine appeal with a tuxedo shirt, or counter it with a femme blouse. High-quality lined wool will smooth over any problem areas better than a cheaper fabric. Hips should be your first fit consideration; pants should just skim, not cling, where you're widest.

CROPPED

Dressier than shorts, more relaxed than classic trousers, cropped pants have a whimsical but modern attitude. They work with a drapey top or a short, fitted jacket. A pair with a bit of stretch and a straight—not wide—leg is flattering for most body types. Heels make a big difference with this style in lengthening the look of legs; petites should hem the pants just below midcalf and skip cuffed versions.

③

WIDE-LEG

Pants with this kind of flare can look casually chic or dramatic; they're a fashion-conscious choice that requires a bit of attitude and shoes with some heft. They also work to recast your proportions and can be great on curvy girls because the volume at the bottom creates a perfect balance to the hips and behind. Who might not want to wear these trousers? Petites (too much volume) or those who are especially low-waisted.

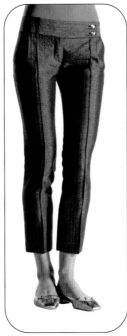

SKINNY

The right pair of skinny pants has the elegance and impact of an excla-
mation point. Find nonchalant glamour with an oversize slouchy top, or
look razor-sharp with a matching jacket. No surprise here: These are most
becoming on slim, petite or coltish frames. They also tend to accentuate
a round posterior for better or worse, so proceed with caution. The tough-
est skinny pants look to pull off? A cropped pair with flats.

how to: **decipher a dress code**

BLACK TIE It's easy for the guys to meet this dress requirement: Don the monkey suit. But while men must wear a tux, women get the pleasure, or confusion, of choosing between several options. To make your pick, factor in geography and the specific type of event or party: You'll likely want a full-length gown for a black-tie ball in Dallas; an elegant cocktail shift might suffice for a black-tie wedding in New York.

FORMAL/BLACK-TIE OPTIONAL Formal dress usually means the same thing as black tie, although in some trendier cities men might get away with a version of the tux that has a black shirt and no tie. Black-tie optional is your host's way of saying she wants a uniformly high standard of dress. If a guy decides not to wear a tuxedo, he should don a dark suit. And you're free to wear a short but formal dress in lieu of a gown.

SEMIFORMAL/COCKTAIL Tuxes are not required, nor are long dresses. But a semiformal evening wedding (that is, after 6 P.M.) would still dictate a dark suit for him and a cocktail dress for her. Daytime semiformal events are slightly less buttoned-up. (The same rules apply if the invite says "informal," a slightly archaic term for semiformal, not to be confused with casual dress.) And similar rules apply to any mandated cocktail attire: that is, a short, elegant dress or unmistakably dressy separates for her and a dark suit for him.

FESTIVE/DRESSY CASUAL They sound kind of fun, these loosened-up mandates, but what the heck do they mean? If you get an e-vite that says "festive" for a holiday party, consider it shorthand for "Make an effort! Wear something sparkly! Show some style personality!" A beaded camisole and black pants would work; so would a full skirt and a cashmere T. The point is to dress up but not to worry about formality. Dressy casual is more of a "don't" kind of message: As in, come casual, but forgo the shorts and T-shirts.

how to: **shop sales**

1   **KNOW WHAT'S REALLY A BARGAIN** An item of clothing has a great price only if you wear it. Write down what holes you're trying to fill before you hit sales. Think about how an item will fit in your look *next* season.

2   **FIND YOUR PAUSE BUTTON** Stop before checkout and divide your would-be sales take in two. And don't compromise on cut or color. Ask yourself, "Am I really going to have it tailored? Is this a color I feel comfortable in?"

3   **TIME IT RIGHT** Most department stores mark down merchandise six to eight weeks after it hits the floor. The deepest discounts begin the week after Christmas. Memorial Day signals the start of spring clearances.

4   **UNDERSTAND THE POLICY** If you're the type who has to take something home before deciding if you really want it, make sure you know the store's return policy with sale items before buying. "On sale" often means "final sale."

how to: **pick foundation**

TYPE	COVERAGE	WHO CAN USE	APPLICATION
TINTED MOISTURIZER >>>			
	Minimal: These sheer formulas can help even out skin tone, but they won't conceal dark spots or blemishes.	Women with clear complexions and normal-to-dry skin are perfect candidates for this barely there base.	Start in the center of your face and blend from both sides of your nose out to the edges, working in sections.
LIQUID >>			
	Sheer to medium: A liquid is ideal for veiling an uneven tone while still exposing flattering freckles.	This works for most skin types. Use an oil-free version for oily skin; avoid water-based formulas for dry skin.	Start with the forehead, nose and chin, then blend across the cheeks. Apply with a brush; blend with fingers.
STICK >>>			
	Medium to heavy: These easy-to-apply foundations can conceal blotches while still looking sheer.	No-fuss formulas like these are great for women on the go whose skin needs a little camouflaging.	The trick here is blending, either with a sponge (ovals are easiest for grabbing base from the stick) or your fingers.

TYPE	COVERAGE	WHO CAN USE	APPLICATION
CREAM >>			
	Medium to heavy: For a dewy look, mix a little bit with moisturizer. But do not dilute it if you need full coverage.	Dry, flaky or dull skin with fine pores is best served. This formula sometimes exaggerates large pores.	Blending it with your fingertips makes all the difference, since you can control how much goes on.
CREAM TO POWDER >>>			
	Medium, matte: These formulas offer a smooth, even finish. You can layer on more if you need to mask uneven tone.	Normal-to-oily skin benefits most from these soft, weightless bases. Avoid if your face is typically dry.	Use a highly absorbent sponge (wet or dry) to smooth on makeup. Replace the sponge often.
POWDER >>>			
	Medium: The newer formulas make skin look soft and fresh, rather than giving a geisha-like matte.	People with oily skin and large pores can minimize problems with a puff. Stay away if you have dry areas.	Use a big, fluffy powder brush to create a sheer look. For heavier coverage a sponge is best.

how to: **nest like you mean it**

1   SETTLE IN FOR MAXIMUM COMFORT Choose sofas and chairs with down-filled cushions; test pieces for sink-in-ability before you buy. Look for sofas with rolled arms that are neither too high nor too low.

2   DOUBLE UP Layering adds instant coziness, especially when you mix textures and styles. Drape a cotton flat-weave or vintage carpet over jute or seagrass. Doubling up on carpets is also a great way to add color.

3   COLOR CODE A limited palette (such as chocolate and blue) works best in rooms where you spend lots of time. Pick one or two hues, and vary the shades. Add pillows for extra color and comfort.

4   DRESS WINDOWS Curtains or blinds are a must for a cozy room. Top fabric or natural-fiber Roman shades with lightweight or sheer drapes for a refined but casual feel.

quick: **tip** -------------------------------------

FIND A DRESS IN 15 MINUTES A good dress can be hard to find: It's the one piece that has to suit every part of your body just so. One style that flatters most (hats off to Diane von Furstenberg): the classic wrap. It works your curves, hugging tightly at the midsection and, thankfully for some, not below. Plus it creates an angled line that keeps the eye moving. Add a jacket, a cardigan, boots or a layering of chains for entirely different looks.

how to: **buy a winter coat**

1

GO WITH CLASSICS A knee-length wool topper with a tailored fit is a true classic that will not quickly (if ever) go out of style. The specific shape is up to you: double-breasted, belted or robe styles are all enduring picks.

2

THINK INVESTMENT It's likely your biggest purchase of the season, so budget accordingly. And be willing to go on a few shopping trips to find the perfect one—a coat is the rare garment from which you can demand perfection.

3

MAKE IT A CLOSE FIT You want the closest fit possible (higher armholes, for instance, are always hipper than billowing ones) but one that gives you absolutely no difficulty in getting the coat on and off or buttoning it.

4

LOOK BEHIND Don't forget the rear view. Some shape to a coat is good, but you should never see an outline of any proverbial junk in the trunk—the coat should glide over any problem areas and have movement in back.

5 **WATCH FOR DRAPE** A coat should not only button easily across your chest; it should also fall in a straight line from the lowest button to the bottom hem, a sign that it's well cut and has ample fabric to suit your hips.

6 **CHECK THE HEM** Do you wear skirts or dresses a lot? Take into account not only how they will look with the length of the coat you're buying, but also how the proportion and shape of the coat will work with them.

7 **FACTOR IN LAYERS** Also consider the clothes you'll typically wear underneath. If you need the coat to cover a suit jacket, bring one with you when you shop.

8 **TAKE A SEAT** Finally, your coat should "sit" well. So button it up and park yourself in the dressing room. Do you have two laps? Do the closures pull? They shouldn't.

how to: **be stocked and ready for drinks or dinner**

STAPLES FOR ENTERTAINING

pasta
- [ ] two or three types, one of them green

rice
- [ ] one long grain
- [ ] one short grain
- [ ] arborio for risotto

stocks (for soups)
- [ ] beef
- [ ] chicken
- [ ] vegetable

spreadables
- [ ] grainy mustard
- [ ] dijon mustard
- [ ] olive tapenade
- [ ] sun-dried-tomato tapenade
- [ ] artichoke spread

charcuterie
- [ ] cured salami

cheese
- [ ] a chunk of Parmigiano-Reggiano

snacks
- [ ] breadsticks or cheese sticks
- [ ] crackers
- [ ] nuts
- [ ] popcorn
- [ ] olives

desserts
- [ ] sorbets
- [ ] ice creams
- [ ] pound cake
- [ ] frozen fruit for cocktail blends

beverages
- [ ] red wine
- [ ] white wine
- [ ] champagne
- [ ] beer
- [ ] soda
- [ ] sparkling water

seasonings
- [ ] canned Italian tomatoes and paste for pasta sauce
- [ ] extra virgin olive oil

how to: trim your bangs

BLOW-DRY

Lightly apply styling gel from roots to ends of wet hair. Using a round brush, blow-dry bangs into your typical style. Don't overcurl with the brush. Never, never cut bangs when they're wet, or they could end up too short.

ISOLATE THE PROBLEM

Section off your fringe by making a part above it, then tucking the hair you won't be cutting either behind your ear or into a ponytail—securing it with clips. Be careful to make sure that the sections are cleanly defined and that only your bangs are loose.

DETERMINE LENGTH

Using a styling comb, divide bangs in half. Starting with one side, gently push down on bangs with the back of a comb and then rest it lightly against your brow bone. Your brow line is your safety position; don't cut above it, and avoid pulling or pressing bangs down before cutting.

GO AHEAD, CUT

Take a sharp pair of scissors and begin "point cutting," or snipping into the bang section at a 45-degree angle. Do it a bit at a time, moving slowly. Repeat on the other half. Never cut bangs straight across: It's too difficult to make a straight line that way and results can be uneven.

FINE-TUNE

Check bangs; step back and check again. If you're happy, you're done. If they're too heavy, cut soft layers: Take a portion of the bangs between two fingers and pull the section vertically above your head. Slide your hand up toward the ends, and let some hair randomly fall. Now lower your fingers an inch down the hair section and point-cut or razor cut about a quarter of an inch above them. If you have face-framing layers, make sure the length is even by pulling a piece of hair from either side toward the center of your face—the pieces should be equidistant from the bridge of your nose.

how to: **buy diamonds**

1 **GET THE PAPERWORK** A good jeweler is essential in understanding the details of quality. For any diamond that is over 1 carat, he should provide a certificate that outlines exact weight and gives scores for cut, color and clarity.

2 **EYEBALL THEM** Check for sparkle: Well-cut facets increase the amount of light that will pass through a stone. Also look for an absence of color, plus plenty of clarity— the best stones are free of any tints, spots or chips.

3 **WEIGH YOUR PURCHASE** Carats measure a diamond's size. A 1-carat solitaire diamond ring can cost 10 times more than a ring with smaller diamonds weighing 1 carat total because smaller stones are more common.

4 **CONSIDER THE SURROUNDINGS** Platinum or white-gold mountings enhance a diamond's white color. Channel settings are the most expensive; diamonds held by a band or by prongs cost less.

how to: **get smoother skin**

WASH Dry skin? Not what we'd call simply irresistible. If your skin is less than glowing, you may be over-cleansing with a soap that dries or irritates your skin and removes its natural moisture barrier. Especially if your skin is sensitive, try a "soap free" liquid product or a glycerin soap instead. And keep your shower tepid—and short. While cold water won't dissolve the substances in soap well enough to get you completely clean, lingering for more than 10 to 15 minutes will suck moisture from your skin.

EXFOLIATE We recommend at least weekly exfoliation to keep your skin smooth. Scrub skin while it's dry, before showering, so your product doesn't wash away before it has done its sloughing. Give special attention to rough, dry areas like the elbows, knees and backs of heels by exfoliating with a body brush in gentle, circular motions. And don't forget your back. If you have sensitive skin, skip possibly irritating scrubs and exfoliate with a wash that contains glycolic or salicylic acid instead.

MOISTURIZE Stock up on the economy sizes of body lotion and, if you want truly baby-smooth skin, apply lotion at least twice a day. If your feet are especially dry, put on socks after you moisturize at night to seal in moisture while you sleep. And always lube up after shaving or showering; applying lotion to damp, plumped-up skin will seal in the most hydration. To hide cellulite, consider a body moisturizer with self-tanner, or follow your moisturizer with a hydrating body oil, since the instant sheen will distract from any imperfections. Also consider purchasing an arsenal of different products: Try a body lotion with SPF for day, an in-shower moisturizer to save time after your workout, and a no-frills formula for night.

 DID YOU KNOW? The human body sheds approximately 150,000 cells a day.

how to: **arrange a living room**

SOFA A seat height of 15 to 18 inches and depth of 24 to 32 inches is standard. If the sofa will be for napping, look for one at least seven feet long. But aim to have your sofa occupy no more than 25 percent of your total floor space.

ARTWORK If it's hanging above the sofa, it should generally be about half the sofa's length so as not to seem too overpowering.

END TABLE You want to be able to rest your drink there with ease. It should be about the same height and depth as the arms of the sofa or chair beside it.

COFFEE TABLE Make it around the same height as the sofa seat. You don't want to have to reach too far down to get a magazine or glass. Low heights in a sofa or coffee table feel modern and can help to make a space seem taller.

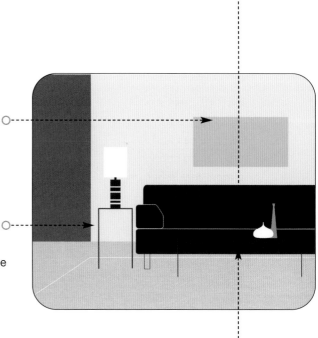

how to: **arrange a dining room**

CHANDELIER The diame- ○ ter of a dining room fixture should be roughly 15 inches smaller than the width of a rectangular table. The bottom of the chandelier should hang between 30 and 36 inches above the table.

DOORS There are two ○ standard heights: six feet eight inches and seven feet. Going shorter makes a room feel larger, as architect Frank Lloyd Wright was famous for doing.

ARTWORK Key words: ○ eye level. Hang it about five feet above the floor; when in doubt, go lower.

WINDOW TREATMENTS ○ Floor-to-ceiling drapes should just graze the floor and are usually hung from a rod placed four to six inches above the top of the window frame. For a more dramatic effect, hang the curtains higher—just below the crown molding.

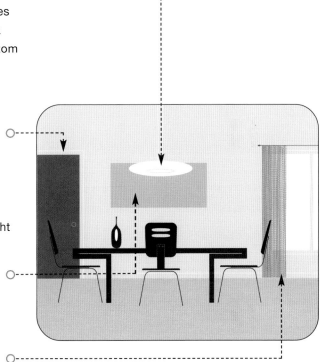

how to: **recognize quality**

1 **EXPERIMENT** If you're in the market for an investment purchase like a suit or coat, try on the very best you can find—not to tempt yourself into a purchase you can't afford, but to get a sense of how a garment should ideally feel, hang and drape. This will give you an idea of what to imitate at lower price points.

2 **SEDUCED BY LABELS?** A designer label can indicate quality. But more important than who made the garment is *how* it was made.

3 **KNOW YOUR FABRICS** Great fabric begets great clothes. Sure, 100 percent cashmere, wool or silk is a safe bet. Harder to judge are the myriad mixes out there. In general, beware any sheen on suits or jackets, and skip microfibers that feel rough to the skin. If something looks wrinkled on the hanger, leave it there.

4 **CHECK SEAMS, HEMS AND STITCHING** A good hem is double-stitched and invisible from the outside of the garment. A generous fabric allowance is another good sign. Also look at seams: They should be straight—no pulling or puckering. And the stitches themselves should be secure and even; steer clear of anything that looks more like basting than small and careful stitching.

5 **TEST ZIPPERS AND BUTTONS** Try any zippers a few times. And make sure the buttons seem secure but aren't sewn on so tightly that they'll pop off when you use them. Look at the buttonholes too. They're not shedding lots of threads, are they?

6 **LOOK AT LININGS** The best add substantially to a jacket or coat's feel and ease of wear, and they're usually made of silk. But you can still have a higher-quality garment with a less fancy rayon or acetate; most important is that the lining be sewn in straight so as not to harm the way the piece hangs.

how to: **do shimmer right**

1 CHOOSE YOUR SHADE Make sure the highlighter you're using looks as if it melts into your skin. Roughly, silvery or platinum shades suit fair, porcelain complexions. Light to medium skin looks most radiant and healthy in pale roses or golds. If you have brown skin, go for bronze tones.

2 GLEAM ON Test shimmer first on your hand to make sure you've got the right product. It should have a soft, even gleam, not chunks of glitter.

3 LAYER IT If you're layering shimmer on top of foundation, don't use a sponge, since it can remove base. Instead, use fingers with a cream and a soft brush with powder.

4 MAKE EYES POP A little highlighter under the arches of the brows can make eyes look bigger, but be sure you don't choose a shade that's too white. The best shade for very light complexions is pearly with a touch of gold or beige.

5 HIDE WRINKLES To downplay wrinkles and make dry skin look smooth and poreless, apply a thin layer of understated shimmer under foundation.

6 CREATE A PUCKER To make lips poutier, use a small brush to apply a dab of loose shimmer powder to the Cupid's bow (the V-shaped indent on the upper lip) and the center of the bottom lip.

7 USE CREAM OR POWDER? Shimmer comes in lots of formulas, for many purposes. Creams, which make skin look dewy, work best on normal to dry complexions. Powders have the highest wattage because they lack the dulling binders that keep pigment pressed into a cream or liquid.

how to: **choose sunglasses**

1 **BE FUSSY ABOUT FIT** If you have smaller features, you don't necessarily need tiny frames, but make sure that any larger shapes sit high on your nose and that the frames don't extend beyond the sides of your face.

2 **CHECK OUT THE BRIDGE** To shorten the look of your nose, choose a style with a bridge that sits lower. (Skip frames in which the bridge is level with the top of the glasses.) Your eyebrows should peek out above the top.

3 **SEEK COLOR CONTRAST** In a colored frame or tinted lens, start with the colors that usually flatter you in makeup or clothes. But within that group, skip shades that most closely match your skin tone.

4 **WORK AGAINST FACE SHAPE** Square faces look right in frames with rounded corners. Round faces do well with more angular shapes. Oval faces can wear a variety of styles.

how to: **look better in photos**

1   FACE To avoid looking as if you have a double chin, straighten your neck, relax your shoulders, then push your chin out and slightly downward.

2   HAIR Traditional updos can look severe on film. To soften features, either leave your hair down or do a partial updo, letting hair in front fall forward to frame your face.

3   SMILE A model's advice: Place the tip of your tongue behind your top front teeth as you smile to relax facial muscles and (further) avoid the double chin.

4   ARMS Prevent sausage press: Never rest your arms against your torso; angle them back from your body (or cover up with a lace shawl or sleeves).

5   DRESS Solid, dark colors are always the most slimming. Dipping necklines are flattering too. To focus attention on your upper body, wear something clingy.

6 FEET A red-carpet rip-off: Position one foot in front of the other, swivel your hips, and turn feet slightly away from the camera to narrow and lengthen your image.

7 SKIN Foundation is a must, as is cover-up, for undereye circles. Natural light in a shady outdoor area is more forgiving than direct sun or a flash.

8 HEAD Try to think of something pleasant and stay focused on the camera. An authentic smile makes for a better photo than an empty one.

9 HANDS Point them down around the edges of your hips to make that area look smaller. If you're holding a drink, put it down.

10 DIAPHRAGM Breathe out just before the shot to relax your face and body. Breathing in can raise your shoulders slightly.

how to: **choose a face mask**

PROBLEM	WHAT TO LOOK FOR	HOW TO USE

DRY SKIN >>>

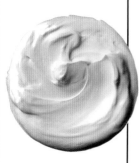

Creamy formulas with ingredients that retain water, such as hyaluronic acid and glycerin, are best. Products with vitamin E and olive oil can also help keep moisture sealed into skin.

This kind of mask doesn't contain irritants, so you can use it as often as you wish. Apply to the whole face, in-cluding sensitive eye and mouth areas. And don't forget the neck.

FINE LINES >>

A moisturizing for-mula that includes retinol, glycolic acid or peptides works well on skin that's been damaged by time or tanning. No mask will eliminate wrinkles, but these ingredients can temporarily plump up skin and make it look smoother.

Glycolic acid can irritate skin, so do not use these masks more than two times a week— and avoid eye and mouth areas. Apply evenly to the rest of the face and other spots—such as the tops of hands—that are similarly prone to sun damage.

PROBLEM	WHAT TO LOOK FOR	HOW TO USE
ACNE-PRONE SKIN >>		
	You need anti-inflammatory ingredients like salicylic acid (which exfoliates and cleans out pores) and formulas with benzoyl peroxide and sulfur, which kill bacteria.	Use once a week to avoid drying out skin, and apply to wherever you usually break out— whether that's the T-zone or all over (but avoid eye and mouth areas).
ROSACEA/REDNESS >>>>>>>>>>>>>>>>>>>>>>>>>>>>>>>>>>>>>		
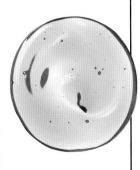	Calming ingredients like aloe vera, chamomile, cucumber, maple and green tea will reduce redness and inflammation temporarily. Formulas with sulfur, licorice-root extract and xanthine can help constrict visible capillaries.	Start by applying once a week. If it works, you can bump it up to twice a week. These masks are gentle and can be applied all over the face. To remove the mask, use your fingers. They're less irritating than a washcloth.

how to: **dress for your body**

issue: **pear-shaped**

To downplay a larger bottom, emphasize your upper body with clothes that have strong shoulders. You could try a structured jacket (avoid anything with actual shoulder pads) or an off-the-shoulder or wide scoop-neck top. Both options help create a horizontal line across the shoulders that balances out curves below. Wearing texture or details on top will also draw the eye up. Skirts can be another easy option for you; an A-line shape offers subtle camouflage, and a full skirt with a well-defined waist can work too.

issue: **short-waisted**

A long top with a short skirt is one solution. A dress with an Empire waist (one that sits above your natural waist) is almost universally flattering. Eliminating the waistband of a skirt (or choosing styles without one) can elongate your body and narrow the line across the hips. A belt also offers an easy way to move your waist up or down. (In your case you'll want a wide style that hits just above your hips when you wrap it around a knit dress or buckle it over a blouse. Generally avoid looping anything around your natural waist.) With pants, those that hit halfway between the belly button and pelvic area help a short waist.

issue: **long-waisted**

To downplay the length of your torso, wear tops that sit right at the waistband and are either blousy or shapely. A silk blouse with a tying sash can work well; so can a shorter sweater that narrows to a wide band. Avoid short and boxy tops. Long waists can also get a visual boost from wide-leg pants that have a natural waist (for obvious reasons, avoid low-riders). Wear with heels, which elongate the legs.

issue: **short**

Your goal is to create an unbroken line that gives the illusion of stature.
Wearing one color from head to toe accomplishes that mission; so do
tailored pieces without a lot of volume. If you long for a little volume,
you're generally safer with a blouson than a circle skirt. And the sleeker
you can go on the bottom, the more options you have for fullness up top.
Of course, heels help, and you should have your pants hemmed with a
pair of specific shoes in mind (the longer you can leave your trousers,
the better). But don't wear heels that are so high you look off-balance; it
takes a long leg to handle three-inch spikes.

issue: **boyish**

Got a push-up bra? It can do wonders to create a little more oomph with
evening wear. You can create some curves below with a straight skirt that
hits just above the knees and is a bit pegged—that is, sloping in as it
goes from hips to knees. A wide belt sitting on your hip bones can also
create shape. And look for fabrics and cuts with movement, like jersey,
silk, bias cuts and pleats.

issue: **full-bosomed**

While a scoopneck isn't your best neckline, a V can be quite flattering,
even if it shows a bit of cleavage. If you're more modest layer a dark color
beneath a gray V-neck sweater: You'll create a minimizing optical illusion.
If you're more comfortable in higher necklines, something square can be
flattering, since it shows off your collarbone. You can also employ the
classic colorblocking approach, wearing a darker color on top than you
do on the bottom, to draw attention away from your bosom. For similar
reasons you'll get a lot of use out of a fitted black blazer.

how to: get summer style to go

BASICS FOR YOUR NEXT BEACH TRIP

❏ **tunic** It will double as your beach cover-up and as a daytime dress.

❏ **jersey dress** Packs like a dream; can be dressed up for evening

❏ **metallic thong sandals** Like flip-flops, but so much more versatile

❏ **black cardigan** For your shoulders on chilly nights and for getting there on the plane

❏ **sarong** Find one with enough fabric to make it into a dress: Tie above your bust in front, take ends in hands and then tie again, halter-style, around your neck.

❏ **full, crinkly skirt** Packable and great for sightseeing

❏ **tank** For the beach, or with a skirt

❏ **fitted cotton blazer** A little warmth and polish to wear over layers

❏ **long, tailored shorts** Wear with a T for day, or dress up with heels for night.

❏ **yoga pants** For walks on the beach, and (because of the flare) more flattering than sweats

❏ **beach bag** Let it double as your carry-on, and find a clutch that fits easily inside.

❏ **hat** Your skin will thank you.

❏ **jewelry** Three pieces should do: Try a big, inexpensive cuff, long earrings and cheap studs.

quick: tip

DROP FIVE POUNDS WITH A CANDY BAR IN HAND
Stand up straight. Aligning your spine makes you look thinner, because it causes your belly to tighten and your butt to tuck under. Focus on lifting your abdomen and rib cage more than on throwing back your shoulders.

how to: **set a clothing budget**

1 **KNOW YOUR INCOME** Figure out your household's annual take-home pay—that is, the money left after federal, state and local taxes are paid and any other deductions are taken out.

2 **FIND YOUR CLOTHING BUDGET** Now divide by 10: This is the amount you don't want to go beyond when buying clothes.

3 **HALVE THAT AMOUNT** This is what you've got to work with for fall/winter or spring/summer clothes, including a little wiggle room.

4 **FIGURE IN BIG ITEMS** Think about big-ticket clothes and accessories, the things you know you'll be spending more on this year, like a new wool coat, an interview suit, a bridesmaid dress or a leather handbag. Jot down estimated prices for those.

5 **DO THE MIDPRICED ITEMS** Write down estimated prices for a capsule wardrobe (the bare-bones building blocks) for each season, plus shoes.

6 **COMPUTE YOUR TOTAL** What's left? This has to cover any accessories, underwear, trendier impulse items, plus athletic and travel gear. Are you in the red? Go back, starting with the big-ticket items, and figure out what you can get for less.

7 **KEEP A SHOPPING JOURNAL** To try to keep the financial discipline going, make a point of writing down all of your clothing or accessory purchases. It's like keeping a food journal when you want to diet: You'll quickly see your weak spots.

 A typical woman shops for about 25,184 hours over 63 years.

how to: **choose a white shirt**

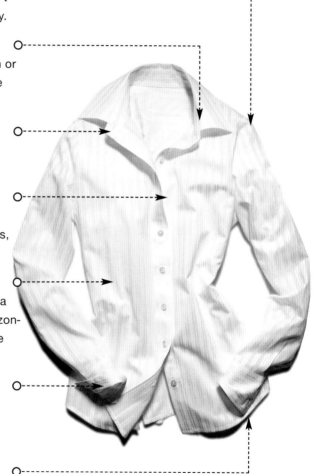

CUT You want tailored perfection—a shape that isn't too loose, boxy or billowy.

FABRIC A collared white shirt works best in poplin or twill, which give structure and aren't too sheer.

COLLAR One that's too tall (and stiff) will rub against your neck.

FRONT Watch for any pulling across the chest, gaps between the buttons, or lift at the front hem.

DARTS Vertical darts below the bust help give a shirt a tailored look. Horizontal darts to the side of the bust accentuate curves.

CUFFS French cuffs add flair, but make sure they fall no farther than just past your wristbone.

LENGTH For most, a hem that hits about an inch below the waistline will look best.

how to: **look well-rested**

1   **LIE DOWN AGAIN** Reduce eye bags by lying down with slices of cold, raw potato over your eyes. A brewed tea bag soaked overnight in cold milk will also work.

2   **WAKE UP YOUR FACE** Reduce bloating with a washcloth soaked in icy water. And put your moisturizer in the fridge—a cold cream can help constrict blood vessels.

3   **GET MOVING** Try using a jump rope for three to five minutes. Don't overload on caffeine to combat fatigue; drink your normal amount, then drink water all day to rehydrate.

4   **ADD SOME GLOW** Splash on cold water spiked with witch hazel or lavender oil. Massage your face to promote circulation. Then smooth on tinted moisturizer.

5   **FOCUS ON EYES** Tilt your head down a bit as you apply concealer so you can see the areas of shadow to cover. Curl lashes to make eyes look bigger and more awake.

how to: **shape your brows**

TRIM STRAY HAIRS

Shape is the big factor in making your brows a major asset, but looking tidy matters too. So invest in a pair of brow scissors, and trim hair to a uniform length. Using a brow brush or clean mascara wand, comb a section of your brow up to just above the brow line, then trim errant hairs.

FIND THE INNER EDGE

Grab a brow pencil (if you don't have one, any pencil will do) and lay it vertically along the right side of your nose; where the point hits should be the starting point of your ideal brow. Mark the spot and tweeze only outside the pencil's edge, or you will risk making your nose look wider.

LOCATE THE ARCH

Next, hold the pencil at the outside of the iris. Where this point lines up with your brow should be the pinnacle of the arch, and, in a few more steps, you'll be tweezing with this shape in mind. But remember, slightly more natural brows are in style now. You don't want to shoot for something too skinny or dramatically arched.

FIND THE OUTER CORNER

Now, holding the pencil at an angle, create a line from the outer corner of your nose to the outer corner of the eye itself. The brow should end where the pencil intersects it. When you tweeze, you'll want to make your brow taper just slightly at the end (again, subtlety is everything).

SKETCH IN THE SHAPE

Using a brow liner, dark eye shadow or some brow powder and a round brush, lightly sketch in your ideal eyebrow shape based on the points measured in the steps above (when in doubt, leave it thicker). Use a white pencil or a concealer stick to mark any stray hairs that fall outside the measured points.

TWEEZE

Now you'll fine-tune the brow shape you've outlined in white. Take your time and be precise; removing one hair at a time avoids mistakes. As you go, step back and look at the shape and balance from a distance; keep in mind that people tend to overpluck on their dominant side.

how to: **set a proper table**

1

FORKS Dinner guests will start with utensils placed on the outside and work their way in, so put the salad fork the farthest from the place setting, entrée fork closest.

2

KNIFE AND SPOONS The dinner knife should be placed to the right of the dinner plate. Next to it comes the tea-spoon. On the outside goes the larger soup spoon.

3

CENTERPIECE Colorful, seasonal fruits are beautiful, easy and conducive to conversation. Tightly massed, short arrangements of a single flower also work.

4

PLATES The old rule was that dinner plates didn't go on the table before the food was served (a charger was used instead). Rules change. Bread plates go above the forks.

5

GLASSWARE Always on your right. Water goblet is above the dinner knife. The red wineglass is larger than the white.

how to: **match your shoes to your outfit**

(1)

WITH A SLIM SKIRT

Wearing a pencil? Sleek pumps or kitten (also called princess) heels with pointy toes are the way to go. Flattering to any leg, these classy picks match the sexy feel of the skirt without being overt. The slightly lower heel, in particular, will take you through your workday and into the evening, although a higher heel will make your leg look a bit more shapely.

WITH NARROW PANTS

One of the sharpest silhouettes of late pairs skinny pants with sexy high heels. Delicate stilettos extend the lines of narrow trousers (which can be hemmed a bit higher than you'd leave wider pants) and make legs look longer. Flats can also look cool with some stovepipes but are much harder to pull off.

(3)

WITH WIDE TROUSERS

Flowing wide-leg pants require shoes with a medium to high heel; a flat shoe can easily get lost under any Hepburn-esque trousers. But you want a heel that has some heft; something spiky would look a little too spindly here. For the most modern look choose a wider, stacked heel. (Chanel-inspired round toe optional.)

(4)

WITH A FULL SKIRT

With a swingy, midcalf or shorter skirt, you generally want a fairly small heel; if your legs can handle the lack of contouring, ballet flats look low-key and elegant. Fuller summer skirts usually work with wedges or open-toe espadrilles. In general, steer clear of stilettos (they're too sexy for cute skirts) and avoid very chunky heels.

how to: **apply blush**

CREATE YOUR CANVAS

To prime for a flawless flush, even out skin tone with foundation—otherwise, blush can emphasize redness and imperfections. If you're foundation-phobic, at least use a little concealer around your nose to camouflage any broken capillaries.

ADD COLOR

Smile just enough to push cheeks up and you'll find your apples. Now, using a soft cream blush that closely matches your natural flush and a wide synthetic-bristle brush, sweep color up and outward from about the middle of the apple to the outer corner of your eyebrow. Blend gently.

SET AND GO

Using a puff, lightly press loose translucent powder onto cheeks to absorb excess oil from the cream blush and to set the color. To ensure your glow lasts all night, add another layer of powder blush, in a shade no darker than the cream, on top. Apply with a classic blush brush—with a soft, large head—in strokes that follow the curve of your cheekbones. When in doubt, use less.

how to: **buy a trenchcoat**

EPAULETS If you opt for them, make sure the coat fits precisely at the shoulders.

FABRIC Cotton gabardine is the classic. If you're looking for wrinkle resistance, avoid lightweight cottons; blends are often better.

BUTTONS The best are sewn on by hand and reinforced on the inside.

BELT Updated versions of the trench may not sport all the details of the original, but the belt is a must-have.

BUCKLE Don't bother with it. Simply knot the belt around your waist.

REAR PLEAT Make sure it closes easily. If it falls open the coat may be small.

LINING The warmest removable linings will take your trench from spring through the start of winter. For a spring-only coat seek a light lining or double facing.

how to: **light a room**

1 BUDDY UP Most floor lamps will look strange standing by themselves, so place them within seating zones: behind a sofa, beside an armchair. Torchieres, which direct light upward, are the exception; they can work alone.

2 STRATIFY Imagine horizontal layers: Table and floor lamps should light one level, and ceiling fixtures or torchieres should light the upper level. Dimmers can help your lighting plan adapt to different times of day.

3 GET WIRED To vary lighting or illuminate a tricky wall or awkward corner, try a sconce. Make sure the light source is at or above eye level and where no one will bump into it. Install one or more pendants if you need task lighting.

4 REST EASY When choosing a bedside lamp, make sure the shade does not extend beyond the edge of your nightstand and, for easy reading, aim to have the bottom of the shade be at shoulder height when you're in bed.

how to: **build a shoe wardrobe**

BUILDING BLOCKS
FOR A VERSATILE SHOE CLOSET

❏ **black pumps**
Buy a classic shape
in the best quality you
can afford.

❏ **metallic heels (two)**
One gold plus one silver
equals evening-wear
challenges solved.

❏ **knee-high boots**
Buy a pair in black
with mid-high heels.

❏ **all-weather boots**
Waterproof, with
good traction

❏ **ankle boots**
In a neutral hue

❏ **espadrilles or wedges**
Warm-weather wonders—
they work with shorts,
skirts or pants.

❏ **flats**
Some embellishment
updates this classic
shoe.

❏ **dressy sneaks**
Better-looking than
trainers are for running
errands, etc.

❏ **kitten-heel pumps
(two)** The ultimate work-
horse for trousers and skirts

❏ **casual sandals (two)**
Buy a thong style for
beach trips and a pair
that's comfy to walk in.

❏ **open-toe pumps**
Color welcome;
no stockings allowed

❏ **strappy heels**
For summer dress-up

how to: **make exercise a habit**

excuse: **not seeing results**

Feeling like a hamster on a wheel? You may need to change your routine, since even a difficult exercise regimen becomes easier with repetition; eventually, you plateau and the workout loses effectiveness. To mix things up, alternate visits to the gym with a new class or an activity that offers the kind of muscle variation that machines can't always provide. And do an intensity check: During an aerobic workout, you should feel like you're pushing yourself at a level of seven on a scale of one to 10. If you're lifting weights, choose a more challenging amount. Also monitor your "breaks." The standard time between sets is two minutes; to challenge muscles more, reduce the rest time to 30 seconds.

excuse: **tired and hungry after work**

The solution to giving yourself enough energy to hit the gym before dinner could be to switch to a protein snack, or one that balances protein, fiber and carbs. (Sugary snacks, including fruit, can make some people feel more hungry instead of less.) Use lots of water to wash down your seeds and nuts or cheese and crackers, since it's possible, at times, to confuse hunger with thirst. And be sure to snack before you start feeling ravenous so you're not tempted to ditch your workout.

excuse: **don't have time at lunch**

If you can hit the gym for only 20 or 30 minutes, make it count: Get your heart rate up as quickly as possible during a cardio workout. During strength training, work muscles "to failure" (which means that by the last rep you shouldn't be able to complete the exercise). If you can do more than 12 reps without much effort, add weight. Trainers also recommend adding "big bang" squats and lunges that work a variety of lower-body muscle groups at once.

excuse: **can't wake up in time**

You're onto something. Research shows that people who work out in the morning are more likely to stick to their routines because it's easier to find uninterrupted time then. To try and make a shift to an early A.M. activity, gradually back up your wake-up time in small increments. Start with a 20-minute shift. If you exercise for only 10 minutes at first, don't worry; it's the routine that counts for now. When the new, earlier schedule feels comfortable, put the clock back 20 more minutes. If you still feel sluggish, try forgoing early-morning cardio in favor of strength training. And finally, giving yourself something to look forward to at the beginning or end of your workout (nonfat latte?) can be a powerful motivator.

excuse: **intimidated by the gym**

Buy some workout clothes you feel great in. Clip back your hair. Then turn on your iPod and march in there. Start off on the one piece of cardio equipment you feel comfortable with, whether that means walking on a treadmill or riding a bike. And just stay put for a few workouts. When you feel more confident, ask a trainer for an introductory session. Many gyms offer these for free, and they're a great way to learn how to use new machines or try fitness aids such as a stability ball, which helps stabilize your core muscles so you'll get more out of strength-training exercises.

excuse: **discouraged by how long it takes**

Most experts say it typically takes four to six weeks to really see results, though it is possible to tone up more quickly. The key is to increase both the intensity and frequency of your workouts. If doing a rigorous workout nearly every day for at least an hour sounds too hard-core for now, try adding just 15 minutes to your usual jog and use a few more muscle groups by varying your pace and adding some calisthenics.

how to: **buy pearls**

1

SURFACE Check out the pearl's luster, or glow. The best are shiny; inferior ones are chalky and dull. The surface should also be free of bumps, spots or cracks (or the design should hide them in the back of a piece).

2

SHAPE Contrary to popular belief, oysters never produce perfectly round pearls. Still, the rounder the shape, the more desirable the pearl. (There are great buys to be had on offbeat pieces made with obviously misshapen pearls.)

3

SIZE Price depends largely on what the pearl's diameter measures in millimeters; a mere 1 mm increase can double a pearl's price. The most common size sold is between 7 mm and 7.5 mm.

4

COLOR Pearls come in many colors. You'll find gray, green, black and even lavender versions in nature. To spot a (less desirable) dyed pearl, look for a concentration of color at the drill holes.

how to: **color your own hair**

ARE YOU WARM OR COOL? To choose the right product from crowded shelves, you have to know a bit about your own skin-color type. In general, if you have a cool complexion (pink or ruddy skin tone, with blue veins on the upper part of your wrist), work within cool shades (look for ash, champagne or beige). If you have a warmer complexion (yellow, olive or darker skin, with greener veins on your wrist), try warm shades (look for copper, auburn or red).

TAKE BABY STEPS Stay within two shades—lighter or darker—of your natural color. What that means, roughly, is this: If you have light brown hair, you can become blond, but not light blond. Or, as a light brunette, you could go medium or dark brown, but not black. When in doubt, go with the lighter of two choices when using at-home kits. And don't go by the photo on the box as much as the company's description of the color.

KNOW YOUR DYE If you want to go darker and aren't looking for a huge color commitment, try a semipermanent product. These don't dye hair; they only deposit color. They wash out after about 24 shampoos. Semi-permanents are also good for retouching roots on already treated hair. If you want to cover significant amounts of gray, try a permanent color, which removes pigment and deposits a new color. Results are lasting, so do a strand test to ensure you're confident of your color choice.

CONSIDER STREAKS Highlights are best if you want to add that sun-kissed look or like some contrast with your natural color. And you don't have to be blond to use them. If your hair is black, for example, you can add light brown or red highlights. Plus, roots show less with this option.

 DID YOU KNOW? About $1 billion is spent on hair color in the U.S. every year.

how to: **throw a cocktail party**

1 DISPERSE FOOD STATIONS Foster party flow by scattering self-service food-and-drink stations around your space. Put out a cheese tray paired with red wine at one location, smoked salmon and vodka at another, then crudités and white wine at a third.

2 SET UP A COAT AREA Save time on arrivals and departures by designating a separate room for storing coats and bags; you can rent a rack from a party supply store or caterer for around $20.

3 CREATE SEATING SPACES Rearrange furniture into intimate clusters to encourage chatting. Plan to be able to allow at least half of your guests to sit at any time, with a table surface nearby. Floor cushions, small stools and inexpensive tray tables can be helpful.

4 ADD LOW LIGHTING Set the mood by dimming lights (you can even switch to low-wattage or colored bulbs) and scattering votives. Don't forget some candlelight in the bathroom too.

5 FIGURE OUT HOW MUCH YOU NEED Do the math: Assume people will have five or six hors d'oeuvres and three to four drinks each, and will use at least three glasses apiece.

6 PROVIDE PLENTY TO DRINK To set up the bar for a group of 25, you might provide six pitchers of cocktails with garnishes, eight bottles of wine (assume four to five glasses per bottle), one case of beer, eight liters of flat water, eight liters of sparkling water, one case of soda and 40 pounds of ice.

7 START CONVERSATIONS A great hostess works the room. Introduce people, give them a reason to talk, then flit on to the next person. Don't get stuck in long conversations, don't fight over politics, and don't leave your guests for more than 15 minutes.

how to: **choose a facial**

THE 411	CLAIMS	PROS	CONS
OElXYGEN >>			
A cool mist of pure oxygen is sprayed on the entire face, with extra focus given to fine lines and wrinkles. It should feel like a damp breeze.	Oxygen hydrates the skin, making it look temporarily more dewy. It is particularly recommended for anyone with dry skin, smokers or frequent fliers.	Fans of the treatment say oxygen blasts give them a rosy glow. Many of the facials contain a cocktail of vitamins and nutrients that can plump up fine lines.	Got a hyper-baric cham-ber? That's what you'd really need for oxygen to pen-etrate the skin—which means results are more feel-good than official.
STEAM/EXTRACTION >>			
A soothing, hydrating mask is usually applied to the face, then warm water is misted over the mask; the barrier shields the face from the moist heat.	Steam opens the pores and loosens dirt trapped below. That makes extrac-tions that follow less painful and helps oil-ab-sorbing masks penetrate the skin deeply.	After a few minutes of steaming, skin softens and is more elastic. Exfoliation and warm steam open the pores so ex-tractions are easier to do with less risk of scarring.	Too much heat can cause irri-tation, dehy-dration and broken capil-laries. Overly zealous ex-tractions (i.e., squeezing pimples) can push the fluid deeper and cause marks.

THE 411	CLAIMS	PROS	CONS
CHEMICAL PEEL >>>			
Pads soaked in acid (typically glycolic, lactic or salicylic) are wiped on the face to exfoliate dead, dulling cells from the surface of your skin.	Your face will be left smooth and glowing. Quick, mild peels of about 30 percent glycolic acid are sometimes used before big events to prep skin for makeup.	Glycolics can stimulate collagen production to smooth fine lines, lactic acids can correct brown spots, and salicylic acids prevent breakouts by cleaning out pores.	Burns are always a risk, especially from peels with strong acids and low pH's. Physicians need to closely monitor the procedure.
MICRODERMABRASION >>			
Skin is sprayed with small crystal particles that mechanically polish the top layer (like a sandblaster), while a gentle vacuum sucks away dead cells and debris.	Pores appear smaller, freckles look lighter and fine lines are less noticeable. The procedure is more intense and effective than a scrub because it gets into every pore.	Dark spots can be lessened, but the procedure won't get rid of wrinkles. The process does improve acne, as crystals remove dead skin cells that trap dirt.	The more clogged the skin, the coarser the tool needs to be. And that could lead to irritation later. But keep in mind, microdermabrasion itself should not feel painful.

how to: **choose wine**

PICK YOUR BUNCH There are six main varietals, or wine types, named after the specific grape from which they're made: chardonnay (also known as Pouilly-Fuissé or white Burgundy), sauvignon blanc (sancerre), pinot noir, riesling, merlot and syrah (known in Australia as Shiraz). But there are exceptions to the one grape/one wine rule: Bordeaux, for example, is made from blending merlot and cabernet sauvignon.

CONSIDER THE MENU As with everything, the rules about what wine to serve with what food have relaxed a bit. Still, if you're throwing a dinner party and trying to complement tastes, reds tend to suit red meats, and whites often pair best with fish and chicken.

NARROW THE LIST If you falter when the waiter comes for your drink order, confidently ask for one of the classics. If you want a white wine, you could try a chardonnay (with buttery, vanilla, hazelnut or toasty oak flavors) or, for something lighter, a pinot grigio (described as easy to drink and subtle, with hints of apple, peach or pear). For a red you could get to know a merlot (with rich plum and dark berry flavors plus a velvety texture) or a slightly more restrained and fruity pinot noir.

GET REGIONAL Once you've learned which varietals you tend to like, it helps to familiarize yourself with a few great sources, so you'll know which bottle to select from a long and winding list. For chardonnay, the best sources are usually California and the Burgundy region of France. If you're ordering syrah/Shiraz, scan the list for one from France's Rhône Valley or Australia. Vintages matter too, though learning the best years in different regions takes time.

 There are between 500 and 600 grapes in a bottle of wine.

quick: **tip** -------------------

MAKE YOUR SUIT CROSS TIME ZONES The easiest suits to take from coffee to cocktails boast clean lines and sophisticated fabrics. For evening, play against the menswear shape of the suit with feminine underpinnings. Try an embellished camisole, a bustier or a blouse with ruffles peeking out the front. Swap your day pumps for strappy heels, and jettison the tote for a flashier clutch. Add dangling earrings and you're ready to go.

how to: **arrange a bookcase**

1   PAINT Begin transforming a bookcase into a work of art just by painting it. If you want the room to feel larger, paint the bookcase the same shade as the walls. Back shelves with paint or wallpaper to add dimension. Add color uniformly or stagger backed and unbacked shelves.

2   PURGE At some point early on you have to ask yourself how committed you are to the dog-eared paperbacks of your youth. Does anyone really need to see your college anthology of literature? Consider what you really want to keep and what actually has to be on display.

3   ORGANIZE After some weeding, group remaining books by size (or by color, if it doesn't upset your personal take on the Dewey decimal system). Consider incorporating some horizontal stacks of books to mix things up, as well as to serve as bookends and risers for decorative objects.

4   ADD LIGHTS Once you're ready to show off your arrangement, use articulated lamps (more streamlined versions of the classic two-armed desk lamp) to bring out specific objects. You can also install picture lights on the top shelf to shine down over the whole display.

5 CAMOUFLAGE If you have a section of tattered favorites you want to keep handy, you can hide them behind small works of art or framed photos. You might also consider removing jackets from some hardcover books, since bare spines can look warmer on their own.

6 BE DECORATIVE Alternate sections of books with groupings of decorative objects. If you lack a museum-quality collection of ceramics, don't worry. Colored glass vases in a variety of shapes will fill the gaps in a modern and inexpensive way.

7 USE BOXES Colorful storage boxes from an art supply store will help keep your odds and ends under wraps while streamlining your shelves. Buy them en masse, since having the pieces match makes your space look well conceived.

8 PRETTIFY Avoid putting books of obviously different heights beside each other. Instead, place large books at the bottom of a case, smaller ones near the top, and your most beautiful spines at eye level.

how to: **do a classic chignon**

CREATE A LOW PONYTAIL

First, brush leave-in conditioner through your damp hair until it's smooth. Don't use products that add hold or make hair sticky; you don't want to create tangles or bumps on your crown. Then carefully gather the hair into a low ponytail that sits approximately at the bottom of your ears. If you see any bumps, brush through and gather again.

TWIST AND COIL HAIR

While holding the ponytail firmly, twist hair and guide it into a cinnamon-roll shape by coiling in a circular motion. Make sure to keep the bun near the nape of the neck to avoid looking like an ersatz ballerina and to draw eyes to the curve between the head and neck.

SECURE THE BUN

Tuck the ends of your hair under any part of the chignon, then hold them in place by sliding a clip through one edge of the chignon so its jaws grab both the bun and the hair that surrounds it. Don't worry if a few ends show. You can leave them as they are, or clean them up later.

HIDE THE CLIPS

Push the clip behind the chignon to cover up the hinge as much as possible. Two clips on opposite sides should be enough to secure the style, provided you've coiled the chignon tightly enough to begin with. Extra clips can create a more polished updo, with fewer ends showing.

how to: **choose jewelry basics**

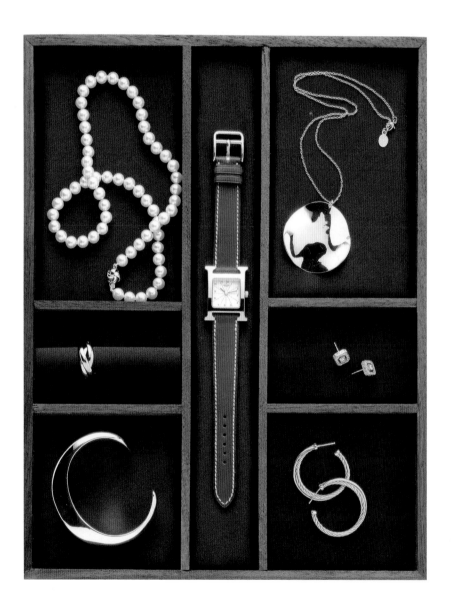

ESSENTIAL JEWELRY CHECKLIST

❏ **diamond studs**
They're perfect with anything and a great foil for more complicated necklaces and clothes.

❏ **pendant necklace**
A slender chain plus hanging charm or gem is a subtle personal accent for work and weekend.

❏ **pearls** Sixteen-inch single strands have serious finishing power; layer lengths for a funkier approach.

❏ **bangles or cuff** Think drama and impact; they're also great to jazz up that cashmere turtleneck or sleeveless dress.

❏ **classic watch**
Clean lines and a simple face make for a piece you can wear every day.

❏ **evening watch**
Make it gold or silver— or add a sprinkle of diamonds on the bezel.

❏ **oversize cocktail ring** Glamorous, extravagant and affordable too, depending on the type of stone you select.

❏ **charm bracelet or necklace** The ultimate personality piece. You can choose gold, silver or a mix of both.

❏ **linear earrings** Longer pairs with a little swing are the perfect complement to everything from a collared shirt to a little black dress.

❏ **long chains** Choose an extra-long gold or silver chain that you can double or triple around your neck to suit your outfit.

how to: fix your hair—fast

problem: misbehavin' bangs

To tame fringe that won't lie flat, add a dab of mousse or spray on a heat-styling product. Then hold bangs with a brush or your fingers and aim your dryer in the direction you want the bangs to go. If they're sticking up, aim at the roots, pointing downward.

problem: limp hair

Put large velcro rollers around your hairline when hair is 95 percent dry. Blow-dry for a few minutes, remove rollers, and lightly comb for volume without much curl. Another lift: Try using conditioner first, rinsing and then shampooing. Baby shampoo also adds volume to fine hair, stylists say.

problem: hat head

Prevent it by keeping hair as clean as possible, since residue makes it more likely to go limp. (You can also spritz the inside of your hat with Evian.) For an instant lift, bend over and mist your mane's bottom layers with hairspray, then flip your hair as you straighten up.

problem: static

Ground flyaways by spraying on a soft-hold hairspray, then smoothing the top layer of hair with a flat brush. Or rub a bit of hand cream into the palms of your hands and run them through your hair. Believe it or not, a fabric-softener sheet (the kind you toss into the dryer) can work in a pinch too.

problem: dirty hair (and you're running late)

Blot your scalp with an oil-absorbing sheet (for the face), then sprinkle baby powder or a dry shampoo onto your brush and comb through roots. Or spritz hairspray on roots and rub hair with a towel.

problem: **frizzy hair**

What makes cuticles lie flat? Rubbing on a smoothing serum, and then waiting until hair is nearly dry before blow-drying. Afterward apply a glossing cream. Flatirons on dry hair also do the trick.

problem: **stale smell**

Alcohol can dry and damage locks, so don't spray your perfume directly onto hair as a quickie morning-after cover-up. Instead, spray perfume on your hands, clapping a few times to dissipate the alcohol, then run your hands through the ends of your hair.

problem: **botched color**

Too blond? For a quick fix comb a gel into dry hair. When hair looks wet, the color looks darker. You can tone down brassiness with a violet-tint shampoo. And if you've gone way too dark wash out some color with an inexpensive shampoo; cheap brands contain more detergent, which will strip more of the new color.

problem: **heat damage**

Slather a deep-conditioning treatment onto damp hair once a week. To make your own: Comb olive oil through hair, put on a shower cap, and let it soak in overnight. Shampoo out the next morning. Every few days, comb in a leave-in conditioner and wear your hair in a ponytail. Try a touch of pomade on frizzed-out ends.

problem: **roots showing**

You may temporarily camouflage with a brown powder eye shadow or something designed for this purpose: a touch-up stick or hair mascara. To draw attention away from the mismatch, go for a tousled style.

how to: **create a five-star bed**

1 **PILLOWS GALORE** The best hotels layer a variety of pillows—firm, soft and neck-roll shapes—on a bed. Do the same and you'll be comfortable in a variety of positions.

2 **THREAD COUNTS** You want a thread count of 250 or higher in a sheet, but beware stratospheric numbers: Some manufacturers twist and double threads to boost the count, so an 800-count sheet could feel thick and stiff, while an Italian-made 220-count one could be buttery soft. So feel the linens before you buy.

3 **LOVE THAT COTTON** Cotton sheets are top sellers for a reason: They're comfortable, durable and pretty. If you're seeking to emulate four-star softness, look for Egyptian cotton or sateen.

4 **TRY A BLEND** Do you like the decadence of silk sheets but hate lugging them to the dry cleaner every time they need freshening? Try one of the new luxury blends. Washable cotton-silk, for instance, can be a practical alternative to silk sheeting. Cotton-linen blends offer the feel and strength of linen without the expense.

5 **FEATHERS PLUS DOWN** The best pillows are filled with a combination of white goose feathers and white goose down. But these pillows are hard to clean, so use a white zip-on pillow protector if you choose this kind of fill.

6 **TOP IT OFF** Make your existing mattress feel a little more luxe by adding a topper between the mattress and the fitted sheets.

7 **ADD A BLANKET** Fine hotels layer sheets and blankets. Do the same by folding a beautiful blanket at the foot of the bed. For something snug and warm try alpaca wool, which has a luxurious feel that's not as expensive as cashmere.

how to: **enhance eye makeup**

1   **START WITH PRIMER** If your eye makeup never seems to stay put, try a primer (available at makeup counters) before applying additional layers.

2   **BRIGHTEN EYES** To reduce red-eye, or make tired eyes look more awake, line the inside of your lower eyelids with a flesh-toned liner. A natural shade is subtler than white.

3   **HUES TO USE** Many people look great in coffee-hued shadows. A more surprising shade that many can wear well? Lavender. It enhances almost every eye color.

4   **SUBTLE LINER** If black liner looks too harsh but brown doesn't seem to blend, try gray. Start at the outer corners and work in, hugging top and bottom lash lines.

5   **BALANCE THE FACE** Strong eyes? Then play down your other makeup, with a softer gloss on lips and a natural color on cheeks.

6   **LINER NOTES** The secret to using liquid liner is to press (not sweep) it on using a flat, square-tip brush along the lash line. This technique paints a precise rim of definition.

7   **FIX MISTAKES FAST** Dip a cotton swab in an oil-free moisturizer and dab the soft tip on the back of your hand until it feels almost dry. Use it to wipe away stray marks.

8   **DOUBLE UP YOUR MASCARA** For long, full lashes without clumps, use two types of mascara: Apply a lengthening and separating mascara first, then a volumizing one.

9   **ADD BRONZER** Don't forget to bronze your eyes, too: Sweep a thin line of bronzer along lower lash lines to make your eye color pop.

10   **GOLD AND GRAY** If smoky eyes are too strong for your fair complexion, try pale gold shadow and gray liner. The effect is subtle but sexy.

how to: **buy vintage clothing**

CHOOSE YOUR VENUE For bargains, shop thrift stores in ritzy zip codes—or vintage stores in less cosmopolitan cities, where things might be less picked over. Call ahead for store policy; if it's a buy/sell/trade store, bring in your own castoffs for cash or store credit. Shopping online can also be worth the time, since prices there are often 40 to 50 percent less than in high-end boutiques.

CONSIDER THE PRICE You can pay hundreds for a pair of cotton Pucci pants from the sixties or thousands for a pristine Halston gown from the seventies, especially if the items have great "provenance"—that is, proof they've come from a single owner who kept them in garment bags for 30 years. But the factors affecting price that you're probably more concerned with are the pieces' current wearability and condition.

DO AN INSPECTION Many vintage boutiques have a strict no-return policy, so carefully examine garments before buying. If possible, give them a once-over near a window, since natural light might reveal flaws that dimmer light won't. And beware the smell of closets past: If the piece has an odor that bugs you, it's best to pass, since dry cleaning won't necessarily eliminate it. Finally, look at items inside and out, checking linings, buttons and seams.

KNOW WHAT YOU'LL WEAR IT WITH Before you buy a true statement piece, have some idea of what you'll pair it with at home. Does it go with jeans? You're done. As for dresses and skirts, straighter cuts (more sixties, less eighties) are easier to pair with existing items in your closet.

A size 8 from the 1950s is about equal to today's size 4.

how to: **apply mascara**

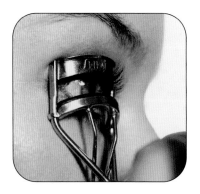

CURL LASHES

The key to longer-looking lashes is largely in the curling, makeup artists say. To use a curler, open the clamp and gently rest the top bar against your eyelid. Don't press too hard, or you might pinch your skin. Squeeze the curler a few times, from roots to tips, to create a soft curve, not a crimp.

BRUSH ON COLOR

To get a clear view of your entire lash line, hold a mirror, tilt your chin up slightly, and look down at your reflection. Stroke on mascara while blinking to coat lashes with more product from root to tip. Want to look more natural? Use a clear mascara instead of color just to seal in your curl and add a little definition.

COMB OUT CLUMPS

Remove any excess mascara and separate lashes with a fine-tooth comb. Gently sweep the comb upward (from underneath your lashes) to preserve curl and lift. Lashes are more delicate and brittle once mascara dries, so make sure to finish this step while mascara is still wet.

how to: mix and match jewelry

1 **EDIT FOR IMPACT** Got a big statement piece going on, like a chunky necklace, metallic cuff or multitiered earrings? A safe approach is to let one stunner be the focus and keep other pieces smaller in scale and impact.

2 **KNOW SPATIAL RELATIONS** Layer it on with pieces that aren't too close to each other: Long earrings and a cuff work better than long earrings and a multistrand necklace. A big necklace and cocktail ring can also work.

3 **FORGET MATCHED SETS** Don't worry about mixing metals, but do make sure the pieces have the same mood. You don't want to wear red-carpet-level baubles with workday staples.

4 **MAKE CLOTHES COOPERATE** If you love bold, big-bead necklaces, consider matching the color of your top to the necklace. The jewelry will stand out, but not too much.

how to: **be sunscreen savvy**

1 CHOOSE A FORMULA Look for broad-spectrum sunscreen with both UVA and UVB protection and an SPF of at least 15. If you will be outside for a while, look for a product with physical blocks like zinc oxide and titanium dioxide. These create a better reflective barrier between skin and rays than chemical sunscreen alone.

2 GET A NUMBER It also pays to understand the numbers: An SPF of 15 gives you 94 to 95 percent UVB coverage, while an SPF of 30 bumps up your protection to just 97 percent. Don't let a high number breed a false sense of security.

3 GIVE YOURSELF TIME Put on your sunscreen 15 to 30 minutes before heading out the door so that the chemical ingredients have ample time to react with your skin and start working.

4 REAPPLY, REAPPLY, REAPPLY Apply another coat after 20 minutes in the sun, then every two hours thereafter. These extra coats reduce UV exposure by 15 to 20 percent.

5 GET FULL COVERAGE It will take about a shot-glassful of sun-screen to cover you from head to toe. Apply clear formulas in particular in small, circular motions all over to make sure you don't miss a spot. A spray can help you cover hard-to-reach areas.

6 BE SAFE Bug repellant, body lotion and high temperatures are all potential saboteurs. And while you should use a water-resistant formula if you'll be in and out of the pool, there's no need to take chances. Be safe and reapply after swimming, especially since toweling off can also remove sunscreen.

7 ARE YOU SENSITIVE? In the summer rethink your wrinkle-fighting regimen: Products with glycolic acids or retinol make skin photosensitive. Try a cream with kinetin instead.

8 REMEMBER YOUR EYES AND LIPS Don't forget a protective lip balm, since lips are also susceptible to sun damage. And if sun-screen bothers your eyes, try a designated eye cream with SPF 15 (it will contain fewer irritants).

9 PROTECT YOUR FACE Look for a smooth, comfortable formula that contains not only sunscreen but also hydrating ingredients. (This will save you a separate step of applying moisturizer in the morning.) Apply to a bare face, with makeup on top.

10 TAN SAFELY If you can't get over your hankering for a bronze, try sunscreen with self-tanner built in.

 DID YOU KNOW? Sun exposure causes more than 90 percent of skin cancers.

how to: **buy a suit**

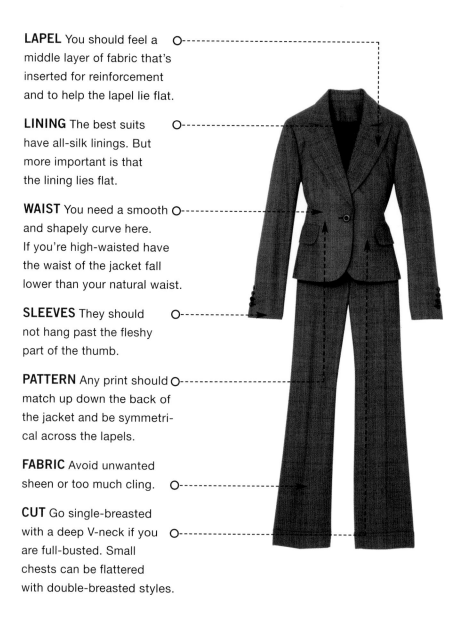

LAPEL You should feel a middle layer of fabric that's inserted for reinforcement and to help the lapel lie flat.

LINING The best suits have all-silk linings. But more important is that the lining lies flat.

WAIST You need a smooth and shapely curve here. If you're high-waisted have the waist of the jacket fall lower than your natural waist.

SLEEVES They should not hang past the fleshy part of the thumb.

PATTERN Any print should match up down the back of the jacket and be symmetrical across the lapels.

FABRIC Avoid unwanted sheen or too much cling.

CUT Go single-breasted with a deep V-neck if you are full-busted. Small chests can be flattered with double-breasted styles.

how to: **care for your skin**

1   **DEFINE YOUR TYPE** Press blotting paper onto your cheeks, nose, chin and forehead. Oily skin will be oily all over; combination skin will be oily in the T-zone; dry skin will be tight; sensitive skin will look red.

2   **BUY THE BASICS** In the morning, counter sun with a lotion infused with antioxidants like vitamin C and green tea, plus a sunscreen. At night, fight fine lines and wrinkles with a lotion that has a retinoid or peptides.

3   **DON'T GO OVERBOARD** Products designed to fight blemishes or wrinkles tend to be strong, which means piling them on may irritate skin. If you plan to apply a retinoid lotion at night, counter it with a mild cleanser.

4   **STICK WITH IT** Most antiaging products take at least three months to work, antioxidants require a couple of months, and bleaching creams about a month. Be patient—and diligent.

quick: **tip** -

MAKE THE PLANE FEEL LESS LIKE THE BUS You can't change other people (or choose their carry-on food, or keep them from—the horror—taking off their socks). You can only change yourself: Stop wearing sweats when you fly. Consider black jersey pants. Paired with a longer top, and hemmed to suit your low black shoes, they can even look chic. And they won't start wrinkling the moment you sit down, the way some cottons will.

how to: **decorate with color**

1   **PLAY WITH CHIPS** If the room you're decorating revolves around a key piece, such as a sofa or rug, bring home paint chips until you find a great match or complement. Then use these samples as the foundation for picking other colors in the room.

2   **MIX AND MATCH** Do as decorators do and affix swatches and samples of flooring, fabric, paint and tile to a bulletin board to see how all of the colors come together. Or bring your samples with you when you shop for other elements for the room.

3   **TONE IT DOWN** Be prepared to downshift. An apple green that seems cheerful on a chip can look intolerably acidic when applied to a whole room. Choose a more muted version of a bold shade.

4   **DO ONE WALL** Painting a punchy hue on just one wall in a room can add drama and dimension. Likely candidates are walls opposite a light source, the wall behind your bed or a long hallway wall.

5   **HAVE A TEST RUN** Once you've found room colors you love, purchase the smallest amount of each and paint a test area. The ideal test is a vertical stripe that's at least several paintbrush-widths across. Evaluate a paint sample under different light conditions.

6   **DON'T FORGET THE CEILING** Moldings and ceilings are usually painted a shade or two lighter than walls, but rules can be broken. A darker color on a ceiling will bring it closer, making the room cozier. A deeper hue for window trim can be an artistic touch.

7   **COORDINATE ROOMS** Once you settle on a palette you love, integrate its colors subtly throughout your house for cohesion. When choosing colors for different rooms, pay attention to the walls where rooms meet and make sure the two shades work together.

how to: **plan your wardrobe**

1   **CREATE AN INSPIRATION BOARD** Make a habit of ripping out pages from magazines with looks you want to buy or imitate. Tack onto a bulletin board and see if any must-haves emerge.

2   **EDIT YOUR WARDROBE** Before you step foot in a store, force yourself to try on your threads from last season, to see what still fits and looks current. Separate out clothes that could work if given alterations or slight repairs.

3   **DO SOME STYLING** Pull out your best pieces and assess what you're missing. Do you need a print chiffon blouse to break up a sea of solids? Are you missing basic black pants? Could a wide hip belt complete an outfit?

4   **MAKE A WISH LIST** Write down what you need and, in a separate column, what you want. Keep your list with you to avoid impulse splurges, and shop for the key items before you add in the fun stuff.

how to: **pick a hostess gift**

MAKE IT EASY FOR YOUR HOST The No.1 rule on hostess gifts is to never choose something that will make her evening any more complicated than it already is. So bring flowers in a vase or, better yet, try a flowering plant or seasonal bulbs in a pretty ceramic pot. The same goes for food: Choose items that can be set aside or easily put out on the table and don't need to be refrigerated or reheated.

BRING SOMETHING TO SHARE If you're headed to a brunch, give the host one less thing to worry about by making a batch of homemade cranberry-nut muffins, or bringing a stack of the latest magazines and day's papers for the group to peruse. At a dinner party, present a beautiful box of dark chocolates, caramels or crystallized ginger to be opened with dessert. Another always appreciated gift: following etiquette by saying a timely good-night 30 to 45 minutes after coffee has been served.

GET PERSONAL Don't feel as if you have to spend a lot on this type of present. Extravagant gifts might even make your host feel slightly uncomfortable. But do take the time to buy something thoughtful and in keeping with your host's passions or interests. A dog lover might appreciate a tin of gourmet dog biscuits. A frequent entertainer could use a box of scented soaps or disposable hand towels. A cook will like a special bottle of extra virgin olive oil or handpicked jars of spices. A tennis or golf player, a season's worth of balls.

CHOOSE YOUR MOMENT Your offering doesn't have to arrive with your party shoes or suitcase. If you're staying at someone's house, you could send a gourmet food basket, case of sparkling mineral water or classic board game ahead of your arrival. Perhaps have fruit or flowers delivered the day after a party, which lets the host appreciate and enjoy your gift all the more. Or go with something simple: Walk over a thank-you note tied with a ribbon around a bottle of the host's favorite wine.

how to: **do your own manicure**

CLEAN AND TRIM

Saturate a cotton ball with remover and swipe it across the nail several times from base to tip. To eliminate polish from the crevices along the cuticle, use the tip of an orangewood stick wrapped in cotton and soaked in remover. If nails are very long, trim them. To make short fingers appear longer, keep nails rounded at the edges.

FILE AND SHAPE

Sweep a fine-grade (smooth, not coarse) file from side to side in one direction. (Sawing back and forth across the entire nail can weaken it, pros say.) To flatten ridges, gently work a buffer across the nail bed in a slow, circular motion.

SOAK 'EM

To clean dirt or remaining polish remover from nail surfaces and underneath nails, fill a small bowl with warm water and mild liquid soap, then soak fingertips for four minutes. But don't oversoak; waterlogged nails get soft and fragile.

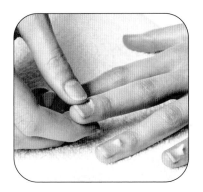

SOFTEN CUTICLES

To prevent cuticles from drying out and tearing, massage in a generous amount of cuticle cream, oil or balm, and let it soak in for three minutes. Softening cuticles this way will enable you to push them back without damaging them.

CLEAN AND MOISTURIZE

Use a cuticle pusher to nudge cuticles off the nail plate, then wipe the surface with a clean towel. Trim off any hard, dry hangnails. Make sure the nipper blade is sharp, or you risk ripping a healthy cuticle. Then massage in hand cream.

APPLY POLISH

Wipe nails once more with remover and apply a clear base coat, which helps polish stick to the nail. When the base is dry, brush on one or two coats of polish, starting with a stroke down the center of the nail, then one on either side. Finish with a quick-drying topcoat to prolong the manicure.

how to: **care for winter clothes**

1 **FOLD SWEATERS** To make sure they keep their shape, store wool sweaters folded in a drawer. Hang only lightweight sweaters (preferably on a wood or padded hanger).

2 **WHEN TO DRY CLEAN?** Pay close attention to the care instructions on a sweater's label. If it says "dry clean only," then heed that advice (and don't forget to remove items from dry-cleaning bags immediately). But pieces labeled just "dry clean" can generally be washed by hand or machine (on the gentle cycle).

3 **CEDAR FOR PESTS** Cedar balls can help keep pests off your woolens when you've packed them away for summer, but only if you replace them often, since they lose their effectiveness after one year. Also, don't store cotton or linen near cedar; the fabrics are vulnerable to the acids in the wood.

4 **TRY SOME LAVENDER** It also keeps fabric-eating pests away and knits smelling fresh. Make your own sachets: Wrap up loose lavender in a piece of cheesecloth and tie with a piece of ribbon.

5 **KEEP KNITS CLEAN** This will help deter both moths and carpet beetles, since beetles are attracted to human and pet hair, and moths are drawn to fabric stained with food or sweat.

6 **GENTLE WASHING** To wash a cashmere or wool sweater, turn the piece inside out, and hand or machine wash (on the gentle cycle) with cold water and a pH-neutral detergent.

7 **HOW TO DRY** After washing knits, roll them in a towel and let sit for five minutes. Then lay them flat on a mesh rack and gently reshape. When they're dry, go over them with a cashmere brush to make fibers fluff up a bit more.

how to: **do a salon-like blowout**

PREP AND CONTROL

After washing, conditioning and detangling with a wide-tooth comb, squeeze excess water from hair. Work through about a penny-size amount of volumizer, detangler or styling lotion. Now blow-dry most of the moisture from roots only, shaking out hair with fingers for extra lift.

DIVIDE TO CONQUER

Separate hair into two sections; twist each and secure with clips. You'll start blow-drying at the front of the crown, since the hairline's the first to start frizzing. To speed drying time and reduce frizz, use a round ceramic brush and an ionic dryer. When you're finished with the top section, pin it loosely on top of your head and quickly start on the bottom half.

PERFECT YOUR TECHNIQUE

Don't make the common mistake of over-drying ends. Instead, start with the brush under a section of hair as close to the scalp as possible. Then have the nozzle of the dryer follow the brush as you slowly pull the brush down the hair shaft, from roots to ends. Repeat until the section is dry.

how to: **care for your bag**

INTERIOR To clean, gently pull the interior inside out and use a standard lint roller to pick up debris. Or try the fabric-brush attachment on your vacuum.

SHAPE Help your bag keep its shape by placing loosely balled-up, white, acid-free tissue paper inside when you're storing it.

HARDWARE Deep cracks or scratches on metal are virtually impossible to repair. But bag and shoe repair shops can replate hardware to hide finer flaws.

ZIPPERS Keep them working smoothly by running a piece of natural beeswax over their open teeth.

EXTERIOR Keep leather moisturized with a leather conditioning cream. If the skin's looking dull, apply a neutral polish with a soft piece of fabric, then wipe with a clean piece.

how to: **fake a tan**

1 DO YOUR FACE If you're using self-tanner on your face, you should always put the most color on the higher planes, where the sun would normally hit first: your nose, cheekbones, forehead and the tip of your chin. Then dilute with an equal amount of moisturizer for the rest of your face. (Be sure to use a headband to keep your hair out of the way during application.)

2 WHICH FORMULA? Cream or gel tanners are easier to control than lotions or sprays and therefore best for first-timers.

3 PICK A SHADE If a company offers different products in lighter or darker shades, choose the one that corresponds to your skin tone, not the type of tan you'd like to achieve. The type of formula will also slightly affect the shade. The emollients in creamy formulas, for instance, dilute the active ingredient in self-tanner, making the color lighter and better for fairer skin. Gel formulations are drier than creams and work well with medium skin tones. And since the drier the formula, the less diluted the color, oil-free sprays often work best for people with darker skin tones.

4 EXFOLIATE AND MOISTURIZE Always exfoliate before you fake-bake to remove dead skin cells that could make tanner streaky and uneven. And then—because the chemical DHA (the active ingredient common in all tanners) tends to bind more to drier, thicker skin—moisturize well. Pay special attention to knees, elbows, heels and toes to prevent them from absorbing too much color.

5 PROTECT YOUR HANDS Wear latex gloves to keep your palms from darkening. Use a cotton ball to put tanner on the back of your hands, and wipe a clean tissue over knuckles and in between fingers to make sure no excess tanner collects there.

6 ADD A TINT For maximum control choose a tinted self-tanner that lets you see where you're applying it. Color guides in some products also indicate spots that need extra blending, then disappear as they penetrate. A general rule of thumb is to use slightly less tanner than the amount of body lotion you'd usually use, and to rub in about a quarter-size dollop at one time.

7 DRY, DRY AGAIN Wet skin can cause streaking. So make sure you towel-dry completely if you shower before you tan.

8 TAKE TIME TO DRY Always add 15 minutes to the drying time provided on the product instructions, just to be safe. You can speed things up slightly with a hair dryer. If you can't wait, don loose, dark clothing, avoiding nylon. And try to apply tanner in a dry, not humid, room for the best results.

9 PROTECT HAIR When bottle-bronzing your face, tie back your hair and dab a bit of petroleum jelly around hairline and on eyebrows to protect them from stains. Apply a precise coat of lipstick or waxy balm on your lips to shield them too.

10 LOOK BEHIND YOU Don't forget the rear view. If you're doing a full-body job, recruit a friend to help you. Products with a mister can help you reach areas like the backs of thighs and knees on your own.

11 CLEAN UP ERRORS You can correct mistakes on small areas like feet, hands and ankles with cuticle remover. To quickly fix mistakes on larger areas, exfoliate with a body scrub. And schedule a self-tan two days before a big event, since any remaining streaks will become less noticeable after two days.

how to: **find a swimsuit that flatters your figure**

MAXIMIZE A SMALL BUST

Underwires, boning, and padding all add fullness to your chest. Just be sure that any padding is subtle and, once wet, doesn't show through. Ruffles, like shirring, can also be a plus, since they can make any area look bigger. (Just as you might not want them along your hips, you will want them fluffing up a smaller bustline.) Also consider the art of distraction: try a top with a pattern, polka dots or embellishments. Finally, make sure the colors of any separates work together in your favor—a bolder color up top and a darker one below will add the right oomph.

MINIMIZE A LARGE BUST

In a top, don't be tempted to go too small: Spillage along the sides will just make the chest look bigger. And keep in mind that suits run about two sizes smaller than your clothing size (honest). An underwire or built-in bra gives structure and support. You can also seek out bra sizing in bathing suit tops for a more accurate fit. And when you're trying on either one- or two-pieces, make sure that the straps aren't a major source of support. They should serve more to prevent sag. A few styles that *aren't* likely allies? Strapless bandeaus, keyholes, string bikinis and demi-bra styles.

③

BANISH ANY BELLY BULGE

A plunging halter-cut suit draws the eye up and away from the poochi-ness below. Having fabric crisscross under the breast whittles the waist; so can details or a bold pattern on the midsection. A busy print also keeps the eye moving so it doesn't settle on a less-than-flat tummy. In one-piece styles, look for extras like a built-in tummy-control panel or a suit with significantly more spandex. In terms of two-pieces, a tankini is probably a better choice than a bikini. In either style, make sure that any elastic in the waistband does not cause belly spillover.

HIDE LOWER-BODY ISSUES

For starters, leave the boy shorts at the store; they tend to make the der-
riere and thighs seem bigger. Also pass on any prints and ruffles on the
lower half that draw attention to the rear. As for what works, a high cut in
the leg can help heavy thighs look slimmer. An Empire waist and details
at the chest, such as colorblocks, light colors or embellishments also help
draw the eye up and away from a heavier-set bottom. And feel free to mix
bikini pieces: Wear a print on top and a dark solid on the lower half, or
white on top and black on the bottom.

how to: **organize your makeup**

1 TAKE STOCK Toss what you never use as well as what's old: Powders and eye shadows should be pitched after two years; eyeliner, lip liner, lipstick, concealer and foundation after one year; mascara after just three months.

2 SORT Organize your cosmetics into those you use every day (which you'll want to store in a handy spot, like the medicine cabinet or a nearby drawer) and those that could be moved to a satellite drawer or closet.

3 ORGANIZE Group like items with like, using clear containers for small items. Leave enough room on shelves so that products are easily accessible and just as easy to put away. Cutlery trays can also help keep drawers tidy.

4 STORE Fill a caddy with supplies for manicures. Put body products on a lazy susan if your supply shelves are packed. And wrap brushes you don't use every day in a soft fabric brush roll so they stay clean.

how to: **pack like a pro**

1   **DOUBLE UP** Fill a makeup bag with travel-size toiletries, cosmetics and smaller bottles of any essential medications so it's ready to go for your next trip. When in doubt, call ahead to find out if you need to bring a hair dryer.

2   **RETHINK THE CARRY-ON** One of these days the airlines will lose your luggage. So make sure your carry-on bag can hold a set of underwear, your bag of toiletries and medications, and any other essentials for a day or two.

3   **TACKLE SHOES** Bring as few as possible, since they're the heaviest items in your suitcase. Place in clean bags (in pairs or, if it helps them fit, separately) and pack at the bottom of your case or in a zippered pocket.

4   **LAYER RIGHT** Put heavy items on the bottom. Place tissue paper between key pieces to prevent wrinkling. Place delicate clothes toward the top, but cover with a T-shirt or other light item. Fill corners with socks and underwear.

quick: tip

MAKE (SEXY) WAVES Using a wide-barrel curling iron, curl random one-inch-wide sections of hair. As you grab each one, spritz with hairspray, then wind it around the barrel. Hold for five seconds; fluff out with fingers.

how to: **choose a new haircut**

GO FACE FIRST The right cut should work with not only your type of hair, but also the specific shape of your face. If you're not sure how you'd describe yours, grab a ruler and measure the length of your face from the top of your forehead to the tip of your chin. Divide by three. That's your first number. Now measure from the bottom of your nose to the tip of your chin. If the first number is smaller than the second, your face is long. If the first number is larger, your face is round. If the two numbers are roughly equal, you're an oval.

MAKE A MATCH If your face is oval, you can wear most cuts. If it's long, chin-length cuts or bobs are ideal because they add width. In general, longer faces should skip the extremes of very short or very long styles. Round faces are complemented by longer geometric cuts that have angled layers; less flattering are blunt styles that end above the chin. If your face is full, you might also want a cut with more volume on the crown than on the sides. Your individual features influence your ideal cut too. If you have a strong chin, steer clear of blunt-cut bobs; subtle layers and playful pieces will be more flattering. If your face is square with a strong jawline, soften the geometry with face-framing layers that hit below the chin, and avoid blunt-cut bangs or too much side volume.

SHOW AND TELL Stylists are visual types. So pull a photo or two from a magazine to explain the cuts you like. If words fail you when you're sitting in the swivel chair, think ahead about how you'd describe the layers you want.

BE REALISTIC If blow-drying for more than five minutes at home makes you tense, say so. Being honest with your stylist about how much time you're willing to spend on your hair can help you find the best cut. And once you've gotten the new shag, ask for tips about how to blow it dry yourself as well as what types of products to use to maintain the shape.

how to: **stock a laundry room**

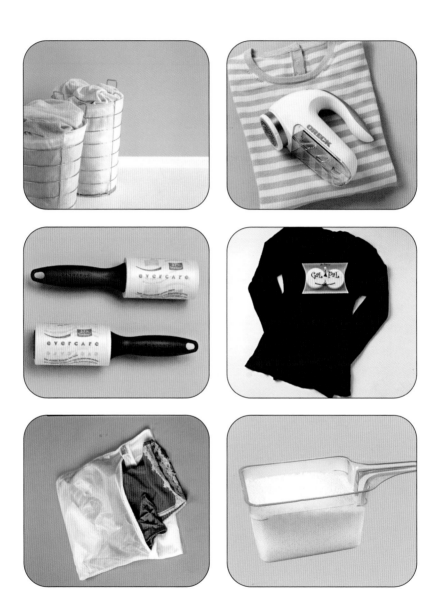

THE BASICS FOR SUDSING UP

- ❏ detergent Make sure it works with cold water.

- ❏ delicates soap For machine-washing lingerie, etc.

- ❏ lingerie bag Pop bras in; wash on delicate cycle with cold water.

- ❏ all-purpose stain remover To pretreat stains on washable fabrics

- ❏ stain wipes Keep a stash to stock your hand-bag for emergencies.

- ❏ chlorine bleach To brighten white cottons

- ❏ nonchlorine bleach For getting out protein-based stains (like blood)

- ❏ baking soda or salt To pretreat oil-based stains (such as lipstick)

- ❏ club soda To pretreat water-based stains

- ❏ drying rack For delicates

- ❏ standard- and travel-size tape rollers To remove lint on flat fabrics

- ❏ velvet lint brush For cashmere, wool and other plush materials

- ❏ clothing brush For coats and sturdy wool garments

- ❏ crochet hook To fix snags

- ❏ antistatic spray To prevent cling

- ❏ coarser pantyhose To remove deodorant stains in a pinch

how to: **choose accessories**

1 **ADD IMPACT WITH JEWELRY** Amazing how long, linear earrings bring a silk top and jeans to life. Or how the right layering of chains makes your basic white shirt newly hip. All you need are a couple of bolder costume pieces a season to add into the mix.

2 **BUY GREAT HEELS** Strappy metallic heels can instantly solve a variety of formal footwear challenges. You'll also want to invest in good-quality black pumps in a classic shape, plus another open-toe version to wear with a variety of spring, summer and early fall clothes. Heels in a gem tone such as amethyst or emerald will enliven everything from your best jeans to a little black dress.

3 **BRING ON THE BAGS** At a minimum you need three: a big carry-all, a medium-size structured bag and a clutch for evening. The larger everyday bag should be replaced regularly; these shapes go in and out of style quickly. But a black satin clutch or vintage frame bag can endure for years.

4 **AND JUST FOR FUN** Oversize shades add instant style, provided you find the perfect shape that complements, and doesn't overwhelm, your face.

5 **CINCH IT** And don't forget belts. You'll want a sleek and skinny one to wear around a tailored sweater. Try a thick, tooled-leather version (if you can't shop in Nashville, look online) to wear with everything from your jeans to a tiered skirt. Have it sit just above your hips.

6 **WRAP IT UP** In the time it takes to debate whether pashmina is in or out, you could be at the boutique buying yourself a black crocheted shawl that will warm your shoulders, seductively, at cocktail parties and weddings for years to come.

how to: **set a party mood**

1 CHOOSE A THEME Never underestimate the power of a theme. It can be as simple as choosing a single cuisine or color that will help you determine everything from invites to drinks.

2 WELCOME GUESTS WARMLY What guests see and how they feel the moment they enter your bash sets a tone for the rest of the night. So try to meet everyone at the door yourself—and place your biggest flower arrangement in the foyer.

3 CONSIDER TIME OF DAY Parties at different times of day call for different vibes. If you're laid-back, consider hosting a cozy brunch: Have copies of the Sunday papers on hand and set out several oversize throw pillows on the floor. Make the meal a buffet (try egg dishes like frittatas, quiches and stratas so you don't have to be a short-order cook), and include a stack of lap trays so guests can serve themselves and then wander off to a comfortable perch.

4 KEEP THINGS COZY Chances are you worry about having enough space for your shindig, but the real secret to a buzzing crowd is creating a tight vibe. For nighttime parties in particular, you want rooms to feel full. Try restricting access to part of the house if you have to.

5 LIGHT WITH CANDLES You can't have too much glow (unless you have small children around) for an evening soirée. And everyone looks better in candlelight. So stock up on votives and place them on tables, mantels and windowsills.

6 USE NICE GLASSES Create a uniform look with chic glassware. You can set out simple cocktail napkins and even paper plates, but don't skimp on glasses. If necessary, use one short glass for everything: cocktails, wine and beer. Rent if you have to. A good rule of thumb: Plan on three glasses per person.

how to: **create a bohemian knot**

DIVIDE HAIR

This knot isn't just a great fix when you don't have time to wash your hair, it actually works better with dirty hair. Split hair into two sections. Work a texturizing cream from roots to ends. Grab hair and divide it down the middle of the back of your head (but avoid an obvious center part in front). Create two low ponytails just below your ears.

TWIST BOTH PONYTAILS

Holding a tail in each hand, twist them down and in toward each other. Try twirling the tails around your index fingers to make it easier. Make the twists as tight as you can comfortably stand, since they will naturally loosen a little when you pull them together in the next step.

COMBINE THE TWO TWISTS

Pull the ponytails toward each other at the nape of the neck and gather into one ponytail. Holding the new ponytail tightly, secure by placing an elastic that matches your hair color just below the original twists. To create a loop, don't pull the ponytail all the way through the elastic the last time; leave ends loose.

TUCK KNOT BETWEEN TWISTS

To finish up, you want to lift the loop up and in toward the scalp, hiding the elastic between the two original side twists that are now at the center of the head. If you have very long hair, the loop will be big enough to go through the hole between the twists and graze your neck.

how to: **organize your lingerie**

1 **TOSS AND SORT** Those worn-out items you're dying to ditch? Now's the moment—throw them out. Next, divide your lingerie by type (bras, panties, slips, etc.) and into everyday and special-occasion piles.

2 **CHOOSE YOUR DRAWERS** Ideally you'll want a couple of drawers for undergarments: one for bras and panties, and another for hosiery, body shapers, slips or other items you don't wear as often.

3 **FOLD IT RIGHT** Folding prevents delicate lingerie fabrics from tangling and stretching. Fold bras in half, cup in cup, tucking the straps inside. With other underwear, fold in the sides, then bring up the bottom to make a square.

4 **DIVIDE AND CONQUER** One well-placed plastic divider in a lingerie drawer can mean the difference between tidiness and chaos. Placing bras and panties in fabric-lined boxes also keeps things nicely organized.

quick: tip

DO "PREPPY" AFTER GRADUATION A little prep school goes a long way. Work in sporty staples one at a time and pair them with something noticeably more sophisticated. Wear the fitted polo you've washed a million times with a flirty skirt and heels. Pull on a cable cardigan with skinny jeans and satin flats. Or layer a couple of strands of pearls with a gold chain. It's combining modern with classic, casual with upscale, that makes things feel new.

how to: **find a signature scent**

1 GET PERSONAL Don't know your tuberose from your patchouli? No matter. The best scents are the most personal, those you respond to instinctively and still love after a day on your skin.

2 FAMILY MATTERS To find your signature, first get a sense of which family of fragrance appeals to you. Floral scents are the most popular, with notes of jasmine, rose, gardenia or hyacinth, among others. But you may also gravitate toward scents that are fruity (with sweet but refreshing citrus notes); exotic (more sweet and spicy, with notes like musk, vanilla or ginger); or green (clean and energetic, with bamboo, grass, pine or chamomile).

3 LIGHT OR HEAVY? You'll also want to consider what intensity you want your perfume to pack: Something light is best if you work close to others; a stronger scent works for a night of clubbing. Climate also matters. A basic rule of thumb is that the higher the temperature—and humidity—the lighter your fragrance should be. A heavy scent can become cloying when it's steamy outside.

4 TAKE YOUR TIME Spritz options on blotters if possible, then take a stroll while they dry. The top note, or opening burst, of a fragrance often bears little resemblance to its "dry down" (the way it smells after a few hours), so you'll want to whiff at intervals.

5 GO WILD AND WOOLLY As weird as it sounds, smelling something made of wool between moments of sniffing helps you clear your nasal palette. So bring a scarf or sweater.

6 GIVE YOURSELF SPACE Work your perfume hunt into a few other shopping expeditions, since you don't want to try more than three scents at a time. Any more and the nose gets overwhelmed.

7 TRY, TRY AGAIN If you think you may have found a favorite, go back and try it on the inner wrist of your dominant hand—but don't rub wrists together, as friction alters the smell. Leave it on for several hours before you buy, since it takes time to ascertain how the notes will develop with your skin chemistry.

8 WHAT PRICE? To gauge cost, know that most scents are a combination of natural and synthetic ingredients; the greater the percentage of things like jasmine and Bulgarian rose, the higher the price. (The liquid gold of fragrance is pure tuberose.)

9 EAU DE BARGAIN Eau de toilette and eau de cologne are cheaper options than perfume, since they contain smaller percentages of fragrance oil and higher percentages of ethyl alcohol.

 The average American woman owns four bottles of fragrance.

how to: **conquer your closet**

1 **THINK EYE LEVEL** The less frequently something is worn, the higher up in your closet it should go (placed in a box or folded up between clip-on dividers).

2 **LIFT SHOES** Cubbies are neat and easy to scan, but if you don't have space for built-ins, simple shoe racks or hanging bags will keep your footwear off the floor.

3 **STASH BOOTS** Store upright with opposite ends placed together to save space. Stuff them with shoe inserts or old T-shirts so they'll retain their shape.

4 **FOLD KNITS** Sweaters and delicate clothes need to be kept folded (never hung on hangers) so they don't stretch out and lose their shape.

5 **PAIR LIKE WITH LIKE** Organize skirts with skirts, pants with pants (hanging them vertically, without folding, prevents unwanted creases), then sort by color and fabric.

6 MAXIMIZE SPACE The best closets have horizontal bars hung at a combination of heights; placing the top bar high up in the closet helps use otherwise wasted space.

7 CLEAR THE DECKS Now that you've moved the mess of shoes, store boxes with rarely used items (label accordingly) at the bottom of the closet.

8 KEEP SHELVES SPARE Don't overstuff them; a stack of three to four sweaters or tops is about all you can keep neat at one time.

9 ROTATE CLOTHES There should be only one season's worth of clothes in your main closet. Store your off-season threads in canvas garment bags elsewhere.

10 BUY BETTER HANGERS Whether you choose plastic and tubular or sleek and metal, just keep them uniform for neatness' sake.

quick: tip

GET A NEW BOTTOM As you age you lose muscle tone. To give glutes a lift, try a tip from a top celebrity trainer: Scatter half a deck of cards on the floor and do low squats as you pick up each card. Go down for a slow count of three, hold as close to the floor as possible for five seconds, then go back up for a slow count of three.

how to: **work with a tailor**

1   **ASK AROUND** You want the kind of pro you'd trust with your best suit. But when you're in the trial period, start off having him hem something less dear to you.

2   **DISCUSS RESULTS** Are you expecting a slight alteration or do you want the entire garment taken in? A good tailor will suggest the best means to achieve what you're after.

3   **LOWER YOUR RISK** When shortening pants be sure to leave a break over shoes. When in doubt have the tailor keep them longer. Sleeves should cover your wristbone.

4   **KNOW WHEN TO SAY WHEN** Shortening the sleeves on a blazer? Good idea. Asking your tailor to radically change the proportions of a jacket? Don't bother.

5   **LEARN SOME TECHNIQUE** Ask how he'll be taking in the piece. A tailor can alter a jacket from the back center seam or a side seam, and the latter is often preferable.

how to: **have perfect dinner-party manners**

TAKE FIRST THINGS FIRST At a seated dinner, always wait for the host to begin eating before you do. At a buffet, if you're the first to sit down at a table with your food, it's polite to wait five minutes for a few others to join you. If tables aren't provided and you're balancing a plate on your knee, feel free to dig right in. If you're in a restaurant, wait until everyone's food has been served.

KNOW THE LANDSCAPE Place your napkin on your lap when you take your seat. If you leave the table during the meal, loosely fold your napkin and place it on the table to the left of your fork or put it on the chair. At the end of the meal, set your napkin on the table. Once you've used a knife or fork, it should never go back on the table again. When you're taking a break, rest your fork and knife entirely on the plate. When you're finished, place them diagonally on the plate, side by side, with the handles at four o'clock. Prevent tabletop turf wars by memorizing two simple rules: Your glasses are on the right; your bread plate is on the left.

SHARE NICELY If you're at a restaurant and want to share your meal, never pass a heaping forkful over the pristine white tablecloth. Instead, slide a small portion onto the side of the recipient's dinner plate, or put a bit of your dinner onto a bread plate and pass that. You can also ask the kitchen to split a dish—if, say, you're sharing an appetizer—so it will arrive on two plates.

CHITCHAT At formal dinners there used to come a time when the hostess "turned the table," moving from speaking with the person on her left to the person on her right—a cue to her guests to do the same. While such formality is now rarer than a snow leopard, you should still make an effort to avoid monopolizing one person and pay equal attention to both of the people sitting next to you. When in doubt, ask them questions—polite questions.

how to: **do your own pedicure**

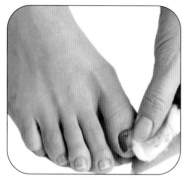

PREP

Cotton balls can leave fuzzy fibers, so instead use a cotton strip saturated with remover to take off old polish. If you're wearing a strong color, press the cotton for a few seconds on each big toe before wiping. Use a dry piece of the same material to wipe clean.

CUT

Next, use clippers to cut nails straight across (avoid cutting from the sides, which can cause ingrown nails). Keep the white edge of nails less than $\frac{1}{8}$ inch long, and don't allow nails to extend past the tip of the toe (otherwise you will risk breaking the nail).

SMOOTH

For a soft square shape, smooth the nail edge and gently round corners with a medium-grade file. Work in one direction, moving the file from each side toward the center; filing back and forth can tear the nail bed, making nails weak and brittle. Then lightly buff the entire nail with a thin, flexible buffer file.

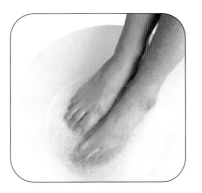

SOAK

Apply a milky cuticle remover over nails to soften cuticles, then fill a large flat-bottom bowl with warm water. Add an essential oil in a scent you like and soak feet for about five minutes.

SCRUB

Use a salt scrub, foot file or pumice stone to exfoliate dead skin on soles and heels, or add a quarter cup of milk along with the oil in the bowl to loosen dead skin. Then massage a rich cream into feet and calves.

POLISH

Gently push back cuticles with an orangewood stick; dry feet and dab on cuticle oil. Wrap cotton around the stick, dip it in remover, and wipe excess oil. Apply a base coat using the three-stroke technique: Swipe down the middle, then once on each side. Add two coats of color and a topcoat.

how to: **buy a sofa**

1 CONSIDER YOUR SPACE Your sofa goes far to define the style of your family or living room, but you want to make sure its presence doesn't dwarf everything else. (And beware: Most look smaller in the showroom.) Measure the exact spot where you plan to put the sofa; if you're placing it against (but never flush to) a wall, you should make sure there will be space on one or both sides for an end table. If you plan to put your sofa in the middle of the room, pick a style that looks good from every angle. In tight spaces, avoid versions with bulkier rolled arms and consider a tight-back style, which is about four inches shallower than one with cushions.

2 SHIFT SHAPES It's a style—and lifestyle—consideration. Do you plan to veg out on the sofa and eat dinner at the coffee table, or will it be used for guests who'll be nibbling canapés and sipping cocktails? Look for something big and cushy to lie around on (maybe a sectional, loose-pillow or rolled-arm style) but something sleeker and firmer for entertaining (perhaps a tuxedo or camel-back). Sit before you buy to make sure the depth feels comfy.

3 CRUNCH NUMBERS Buy the best construction you can afford, since you'll live with—and on—your purchase for an average of 10 years. To do a quality check, lift the sofa. (The heavier, the better. The sturdiest frames are made from moisture-resistant, kiln-dried hardwoods.) And listen when you sit. (The best springs are eight-gauge steel wire set into the frame and hand-tied with twine; they shouldn't squeak.) Then sit on the arms. (You shouldn't feel wood through the padding.) Finally, plop down on the sofa seat near the arm. (The other end of the cushion shouldn't pop up, and you shouldn't feel like you're being sucked into the corner.)

4 GET DETAILED Most designers recommend neutral coverings, since you can always use pillows or throws to add color or pattern. Exposed legs will look more modern, skirted styles are cozier, and metal legs will lend a Euro-chic flavor. Three back cushions say traditional, two look more updated, and a single cushion makes a strong design statement. Back cushions with squared-off edges look more contemporary than those with round edges.

how to: **use concealer**

CHOOSE TWO Making one concealer do double duty for your undereye circles and blemishes is the main cause of unnatural-looking coverage. So pick a thick, dry formula to hide redness and bumps. And find a moist or liquid formula for under your eyes that won't emphasize fine lines as something cakier could. To avoid the Kabuki look, you can also mix concealer with an eye cream containing vitamin C, white tea or green tea (to brighten skin) and caffeine (to tighten blood vessels).

PRIME, BRUSH, PAT If your concealer tends to be gone by midday—or if you have oily skin—improve staying power with a skin primer. Then apply concealer with a small-bristle brush (like a lip brush) instead of greasier fingers. A brush will also deposit the product just where you want it. Always pat (don't rub) to blend, and set your handiwork with translucent powder. And keep in mind that concealers, like most cosmetics, last six months to a year, although liquid formulas break down faster.

KNOW YOUR TONES To cover an undereye circle, choose a peach- or yellow-toned concealer since these shades tend to cancel out darkness without looking fake. When picking a product don't go any lighter than your skin tone, or the concealer will appear grayish. To apply, start at the inner corner of the eye and apply a thin layer over the dark area with a brush. Blend by gently patting with your ring finger. To cover facial redness, mix a bit of green color-correcting tint in with your foundation, then apply a beige-toned (not pink) concealer.

TREAT AS NECESSARY To be sure concealer doesn't make your blemishes worse, choose a product with benzoyl peroxide, salicylic acid or sulfur, which can actually speed healing. Avoid makeup with pore-clogging mineral oil or petrolatum. Brushes, instead of sponge applicators, will prevent cross-contamination of acne-prone skin, especially if you wash them regularly with a brush cleanser.

quick: tip

LAYER FASHIONABLY You want a textured look but one with shape. Layers should be airy and fluid, not clingy. A great base layer is a slim, elongated, featherweight knit top. One chunky layer on top is enough. Remember that even in winter, longer sleeves can be layered under shorter ones for a slightly more offbeat look. Also try a variety of silhouettes in your layering approach: a tunic over skinny jeans or a long silk top under a shrunken blazer.

how to: **buy vintage accessories**

1 **START WITH COSTUME JEWELRY** From faux pearls to Lucite cuffs, it's hard to go wrong with pieces under $100. And inventory is high, so there are deals to be had.

2 **BAGS, BAGS, BAGS** Buying vintage versions sets you apart, and they often cost less than the priciest "it" bags. They may also sport softer leather and weightier hardware.

3 **KNOW WHAT'S HOT** Eighties aviators are on the list (go slightly oversize) as are belts from that decade (seek waist-cinchers). Classic clutches are hip *and* timeless.

4 **KNOW WHAT YOU CAN FIX...** A broken clasp can be repaired. An unhinged bag handle can be refastened. A bag ripped along a seam can be restitched.

5 **...AND WHAT YOU CAN'T** Avoid stiff leather, stains or scuffs on a bag, signature hardware that's damaged, missing stones or beads.

how to: **wrap a gift beautifully**

1 USE FOUND MATERIALS Vintage or new wallpaper remnants trump drugstore rolls any day. Maps or newspaper comics can also be fun recyclables. Or use a photocopier to create a custom wrap from blown-up snapshots.

2 GO GREEN Blooms and greenery make fragrant and festive alternatives to bows and ribbons. To keep a blossom alive, attach florist's water tubes or wrap stems in a wet paper towel, then foil. Use lengths of ivy or other greenery as "ribbon."

3 MAKE IT A SET When giving a group of gifts, wrap them in coordinating papers. To keep a stack intact, stick boxes together with double-sided tape, then tie a ribbon around it all. Choose a topper that relates to the theme inside.

4 PUT CHEERY ON TOP For a new topper, try a bow made from tasseled fabric cord, a fan of chopsticks or petite boxes of chocolates. For a cute touch atop a kid's gift, tape on a rubber ducky, or wrap a large gift with a jump rope.

5 RETOOL YOUR TAGS Repurpose greeting cards by cutting out shapes or scenes from the front and writing on the back. For a fun holiday tag, loop a colored ball ornament through a satin cord, then write on names with a paint pen. Cheerful graphic stickers can double as tape and as mod gift tags.

6 STORE IT You don't need a whole room devoted to hanging rolls of paper and bins of ribbon, but you do need to keep your papers crisp and usable for the next wrap-up. One approach: Slit the cardboard core of a roll of paper towels lengthwise, then wrap it around a roll of your wrapping paper. And store rolls upright in a rolling caddy or pretty bin for easy access.

how to: **sleep like a baby**

WIND DOWN If you're desperate for a little less action in the P.M., you need to switch gears gradually. That means no exercise, caffeine, nicotine or alcohol right before bed. And allow two hours for dinner to digest (but don't go to bed hungry either). Drink more water earlier in the day so you're not catching up on hydration in the evening and forcing yourself to go to the bathroom at night. Finally, set a regular sleep and rising time.

COCOON When you pull the blinds at night, the room should become completely dark and stay that way when dawn breaks. If necessary, try a blackout liner behind your curtains or get light-blocking cellular shades. You'll also want to save your sanctuary for all but sleep and sex; don't bring paperwork to bed with you or watch TV there. If you're a light sleeper, add in white noise from a sound machine or fan.

COOL OFF Set the thermostat to no higher than 70 degrees to complement your body's natural nighttime drop in temperature. But although you want to stay relatively cool while sleeping, you might also consider taking a hot bath before bed. Dropping your temperature markedly after first raising it, experts say, kicks off the sleep response.

GET UP Feeling anxious and annoyed by your lack of sleep will make your insomnia worse. So if you're not slumbering after 15 minutes in bed, get up and do something quiet, like reading or writing in a journal—but use a small clip-on reading light to avoid exposure to ambient bright light, which sends a signal to your brain that it needs to keep you awake. When you feel tired, head back to bed again.

 DID YOU KNOW? About 67% of American women have frequent insomnia.

photo and illustration

©iStockphoto.com/
CampSpot
p. 150, detergent

Bacon, Quentin
p. 56, p. 82

Bartlett, Chris
p. 126

Broom, Greg
p. 14, p. 28,
p. 88, p. 108–109,
p. 136, p. 156–157

Calero, Anita
p. 170

Cook, David
p. 152, bag; p. 160

Coppola + Grande
p. 164, p. 167

Coppola, Christopher
p. 83

Cox, Nigel
p. 29, p. 134,
p.137

Cremens, Kevin
p. 158, p. 176

Durand, Francois/Getty
p. 69

Friedman, Douglas
p. 50, p. 114, p. 154

Gaget, Bruno
p. 58, p. 59, p. 120

Grande, Sabrina
p. 30, p. 92,
red kitten heel; p. 178

Grosell, Nicolai
p. 132–133

Hubbard, Lisa
p. 16

Huffman, Todd
p. 90, p. 128, p. 182

Imperatori–Penn,
Gabriella
p. 60, p. 110

Jarvis, Devon
p. 70, p. 71, p. 107,
p. 162

Koenig, Nikolas
p. 24, p. 40

Kroencke, Anja
p. 62–63

Lawrence, David
p. 92, black pump

Lawton, John
p. 23, p. 48–49, p. 125

Lindbaek, Svend
p. 92, flat with green
bow, black boot,
metallic strappy heel

Loader, Mark
p. 104

Maraia, Charles
p. 184

Masters, Charles
p. 89, p. 42–45,
p. 140–143

McCaul, Andrew
p. 150 all images
except bottom right
of detergent

McLeod, Garry
p. 27

Minh+Wass
p. 98

Mosto, Francesco
p. 55

Muggenborg, John
p. 51

Nesi, Sioux
p. 80–81

Newhall, Alex
p. 172–173

Pearson, Karen
p. 84–87

Penny, Don/Time Inc.
Digital Studio
p. 92, sneaker;
p. 121

Platt, Mark
p. 8, p. 122

Reeves, Ron
p. 174–175

Rubin, Ilan
p. 144

Schierlitz, Tom
p. 18–19, p. 64,
p. 67, p. 78, p. 152,
black pump

Smith, Eugene
p. 36–37

Stratton, Ann
p. 102

Time Inc. Digital Studio
p. 11, p. 15, p. 32–33,
p. 52, p. 74, p. 117,
p. 118, p.124, p. 146,
p. 152, bracelets,
sunglasses, gold shoe,
earrings; p. 180–181

Wade, James
p. 96

Webber, Wendell T.
p. 12–13

object and model

P. 48–49

tinted: Stila Sheer Color tinted moisturizer with SPF 15; liquid: Nars Oil-Free foundation; stick: I-Iman foundation stick; cream: Paul and Joe cream foundation; cream to powder: Cover Girl Aqua Smooth makeup; powder: MAC Studiofix

P. 50

lacquered nesting cubes set: House Eclectic; cutwork cotton pillow: West Elm; table lamp: vintage

P. 51

pillows: Golden Bear at Shelter

P. 52

dress: Diane von Furstenberg

P. 55

coat: DKNY

P. 60

earrings: Kwiat

P. 64

jacket: Chanel

P. 67

sunglasses, from top: Bottega Veneta, Twoeyes, Versace

P. 74

tunic: Patrick Robinson for Target; hat: J. Crew; shorts: Yank; top: Victoria's Secret Catalogue; beach bag: Redfish Design; sandal: Enzo Angiolini

P. 78

shirt: Banana Republic

P. 83

hand-carved pears: Carrera

P. 84–85

from left to right: look 1: black shirt with white cuffs: Trina Turk; black slit-front skirt: Votre Nom; black pump: Sigerson Morrison; look 2: tan suede coat: Express; pants: Shin Choi; bag: Tod's; burgundy pump: Barbara Bui

P. 86–87

from left to right: look 3: burgundy pants: Paul Smith; black pump with velvet trim: Chanel; look 4: skirt: Elie Tahari; purple flat: Calvin Klein

P. 89

trench: Ralph Lauren

P. 90

lamp: Shine

P. 92

clockwise, from top left: pump: Manolo Blahnik; sneaker: Reebok; boot: Calvin Klein; flat: J. Crew; kitten heel: Moschino Cheap and Chic; metallic heel: Aldo

P. 96

pearls: Fortunoff

P. 104

suit: Jaeger; t-shirt: Banana Republic

P. 110

clockwise, from top left: pearls: Honora; watch: Hermès; pendant:

Ippolita; diamond studs: Penny
Preville; gold hoops: David Yurman;
cuff: Elsa Peretti; ring: Cartier

P. 114

pillows, from back: Kukkula
standard pillowcase: Marimekko
for Crate & Barrel; pleated silk
Euro sham: Donna Karan; quilted
blue velvet sham: Pottery Barn;
pleated silk pillow: Donna Karan;
silk pillow with circles: Michele
Varian; bed linens; pleated
silk duvet: Donna Karan;
chocolate sheets: Kumi Kookoon;
lambswool throw: Yves Delorme;
headbaord: Jonathan Adler;
mirror console table:
Urban Outfitters; clock:
Simon Pearce; glass lamp:
Jayson Home & Garden

P. 117

mascara: Lancôme Hypnôse

P. 118

vintage clothing: clockwise,
from top left: shirt: Cherry;
pants: Annie Creamcheese;
cami: Sasparilla Vintage; dress:
Annie Creamcheese

P. 120

model: Samantha/Madison

P. 121

necklace: KEP Designs

P. 122

hat: Scala Collezione;
sunglasses: Christian Roth

P. 124

suit: Ann Taylor

P. 126

pants: Alvin Valley

P. 134

from top: v-neck: H&M; ribbed
crewneck: J.Crew; sachet:
L'Occitane; turtleneck: White +
Warren; cedar balls: Container Store

P. 137

bag: YSL

P. 140–141

from left to right: small bust:
Cia Maritima, Leilana, Be Creative
Shogun; large bust: Fantasie,
Hydra, Shoshanna

P. 142–143

left to right: belly bulge:
Anne Cole, Liz Claiborne,
Jets by Jessika Allen;
lower-body-issues:
Banana Republic, Christina
Swimwear, Vix Swimwear

P. 146

wheelie bag: Kate Spade

P. 150

fabric shaver: Oreck; deodorant
removers: Gal Pal; fine wash
bag: Woolite

P. 152

black pump: Salvatore Ferragamo; bracelets: Fortunoff; frame bag: Sondra Roberts

P. 154

silver tray: Christofle; martin glasses: Crate & Barrel; silver candlestick: Calvin Klein; flute candlestick: Ted Muehling for Steuben; silver bowl: Christofle; glass bowl with gold flecks: The End of History; silver vase: West Elm; The Art of Richard Tuttle: Keena; white taper candles: The Candle Shop

P. 158

bras, from top to bottom: Eres, Simone Pérèle, Le Mystère

P. 160

polo: Lacoste

P. 162

perfume: Chanel No. 5

P. 170

rug, table with plant, screen, dinner and salad plates, water glasses, and dining chairs: ABC Carpet & Home; tablecloth: Crate & Barrel; wineglasses: Conran Shop; cutlery, wood plates, and square glasses with stones: vintage

P. 174–175

left to right: George Smith Sofas and Chairs, Desiron

P. 178

coat: Gregory Parkinson; sweater: Fresh Karma; blouse: Anne Fontaine; necklace: Ashley Kolt, pants: J & Company

P. 180

clockwise, from top left: sunglasses: Giorgio Armani; faux pearls: 1990s Chanel; cuff: 1980s Lucite bangle, sunglasses: Ted Lapidus; belt: Hermès; cuff: at Alexis Bittar

P.181

bag: Chanel

P. 182

clockwise, from top left: #1: Paris map paper: Cavallini Papers & Co.; French chocolates in pink purse: Fachon; Eiffel tower charms: M&J Trimming; #4: striped paper: Eieio; rubber duck and yo-yos: Tah-Poozie; #5: circle stickers: Paper Source; #6: rolling bin: The Container Store; #3: striped paper: Caspari, silk brooch: Vivaterra; #2: pineapple paper: Midori

acknowledgments

kim bello

david e. brown

marina budarina

daniel del valle

terry klockow

andrea nakayama

brian payne

regine raab

holly rothman

nathan sayers

lindsey stanberry

alex tart

shoshana thaler

debra weintraub

betty wong

megan worman

fashion 👜 **beauty** 🧴 **home** 🪑 **entertaining** 🍸

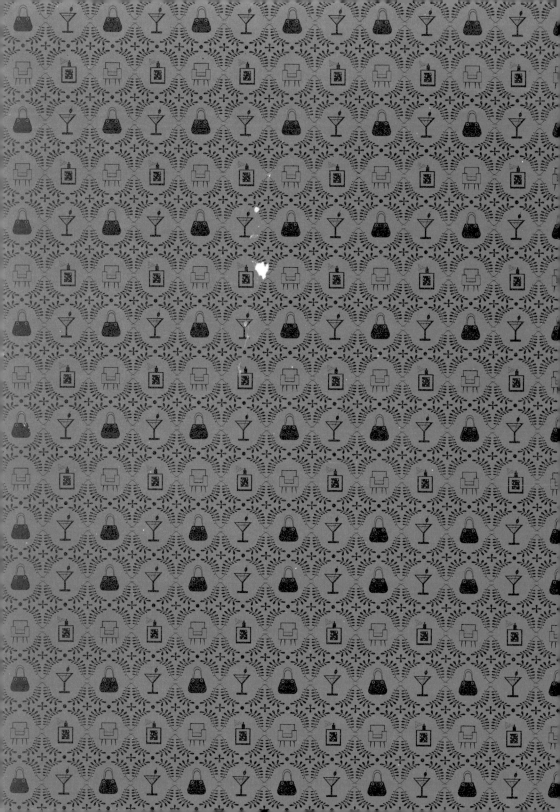